Tim Bowden is a broadcaster, radio and television documentary maker, historian and author. Born in Hobart in 1937 (which means he is now quite old), he is well known for hosting the ABC-TV listener and viewer reaction program Backchat from 1986 to 1994.

He is the author of 17 books including *One Crowded Hour – Neil Davis, Combat Cameraman*; *The Way My Father Tells It - The Story of An Australian Life*; *Antarctica And Back In Sixty Days*, *Aunty's Jubilee – 50 years of ABC-TV*; *The Changi Camera* and *Stubborn Buggers* – the survivors of the infamous POW Outram Road gaol that made Changi look like heaven.

Bowden's background in journalism includes current affairs, news, and feature and documentary work. He has worked as a foreign correspondent in Asia (covering the Vietnam war) and in North America. In 1969 he was the first executive producer of the ABC radio current affairs program PM, before becoming a producer with the ground-breaking television current affairs program This Day Tonight in the early 1970s. In 1985 Bowden founded ABC Radio's Social History Unit. Since 1989 Tim Bowden has been actively broadcasting, writing and researching Australian activities in Antarctica. He was commissioned to write the official history of ANARE (Australian National Antarctic Research Expeditions) *The Silence Calling – Australians in Antarctica 1947-97*. Bowden also presented six half-hour documentaries Breaking the Ice on ABC-TV in 1996.

Tim Bowden received an Order of Australia for services to public broadcasting in June 1994. In May 1997 he was awarded an honorary degree of Doctor of Letters from the University of Tasmania.

Also available from ETT Imprint

by Tim Bowden

Ion Idriess: The Last Interview

Ros Bowden: Trailblazer

No Plucking!

Oddments collected by a reptile of the press

TIM BOWDEN

ETT IMPRINT

Exile Bay

First published by ETT Imprint, Exile Bay in 2022

ETT IMPRINT
PO Box R1906
Royal Exchange NSW 1225
Australia

ISBN 978-1-922698-75-9 (paper)
ISBN 978-1-922698-74-2 (ebook)

Design by Hanna Gotlieb
Cover design by Tom Thompson

CONTENTS

The author as an "oddment"...

Introduction

As I am now in my eighties, I can look back on oddments collected during a lifetime in journalism, a career path I have never regretted. I started in newspapers as a cadet reporter on *The Mercury* in Hobart in 1955, back in the days of hot metal, linotype machines and copy paper. I became fascinated by the possibilities of radio in 1958, when portable tape recorders using ¼ inch magnetic tape had just been developed. This gave enormous freedom to the radio reporter and documentary maker.

Before that, the only way of recording outside a broadcast studio was to cut an acetate disk in a van full of bulky equipment, with a technician.

Amazingly, Australian Broadcasting Commission war correspondents like Chester Wilmot, actually took this highly vulnerable set-up right into the front line, even during the collapse of the Allied effort on the island of Crete in 1941. In one broadcast, when Australian sappers blew up a bridge to halt the advancing Germans Panzers before Wilmot expected it, the force of the explosion blew the needle cutting the disk right off the platter!

My first radio report for the ABC was recorded on a clockwork tape recorder where the sound was electrically recorded, but the spools of tape were driven past the recording heads by a clockwork mechanism. This meant the reporter had to juggle a formidable STC microphone (shaped like a black club with a silver grill) in one hand, and, with the recorder slung on around his neck by sturdy strap, then get ready to wind the spring up with his other hand like an organ grinder, as it only maintained the correct speed for four minutes. Well, a bit less than that, which meant that if you didn't tighten the spring along the way, your interviewee's voice on playback, quickly rose in what sounded like a growing hysteria, until it turned into total gobbledy-gook. There was a lot to think about as well as what questions you needed to ask. Getting all that right was stressful for a rookie radio reporter but it was also exciting.

But I digress.

I need to explain the title of this book. Most men grow a beard at least once in their life. Mine sprouted in my mid-forties in the mid 1980s and a photo of it was taken in Malaysia during a family holiday. Our hotel on the East Coast was near the beach, and a courtyard outside our room was edged by planter boxes containing a few rose plants doing their best to survive in the tropical heat. The following sign attracted my attention:

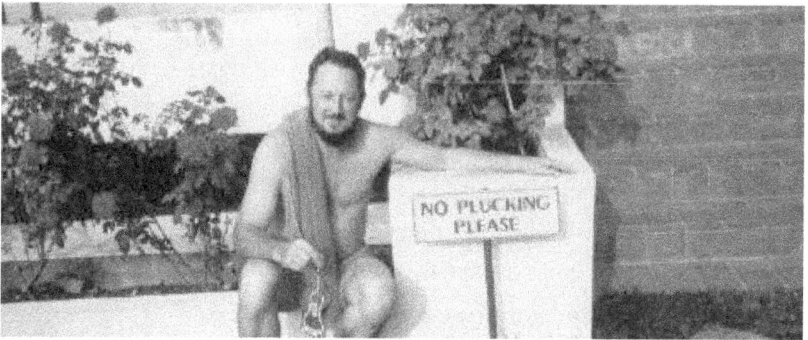

Back in Sydney I was lunching with a group of journalists and lawyers. My legal friend, Jack Grahame, was there. Jack always wore immaculate three piece suits, a fob watch and a silk handkerchief stylishly flowing from his top pocket set off by a matching necktie. He had also sported a meticulously trimmed pepper-and-salt beard ever since I had known him.

Waiting for a break in the conversation, he struck – saying loudly, "Bowden, I want to make a comment about your beard'. The well-wined lunch guests waited expectantly. 'It's rather pubic!' (Loud guffaws.)

I had no immediate response, but when I got home I asked my wife Ros what she thought of my beard. 'Actually, that's your business.'

'But I need to know – do you like it'?

'Well seeing that you ask, not much.'

I withdrew to the bathroom and shaved off half, leaving a half moustache and beard on the right-hand side of my face, clean-shaven on the left. My two sons, then aged ten and seven were watching a cartoon on television in the living room. I walked in and said something to them to get their attention. They looked around briefly, then turned back to the telly without any comment. I returned to the bathroom and continued the removal, and have never grown one since. Jack was right. It DID look a bit pubic.

In 1965 the Australian Broadcasting Commission (as it then was) posted me to South-east Asia as a foreign correspondent based in Singapore. One day a friend handed me the instructions he had been given that came with a Japanese enema kit, written in what might be referred to as 'Janglish'.

The device was quite elaborate, with diagrams of how rubber tubes and flexible bulbs were to be squeezed by the operator to achieve the desired result. However it was important to – how can I put this delicately? – to hang on as long as possible before the moment of release. Which led to the wondrous punchline –'When being unbearable, have a good passage'. Yes indeed.

Singapore in those days still had its original Chinatown, with wooden two-story 'shop-houses', where the proprietor and his family lived above the ground floor shop and sold whatever goods were on offer down below. In this particular case, the Din Medical Hall (Est. 1902) displayed a sign featuring a large eye, with the following message in Chinese and English, SPECIALIST IN EYES AND PILES. It would seem the Singapore population in those days suffered difficulties in both those areas, and it clearly made sense to run a one-stop shop.

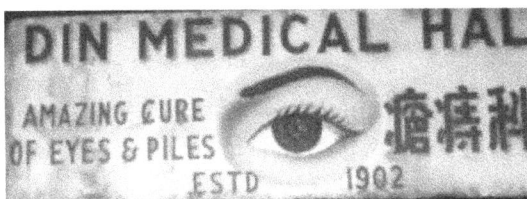

I think that is enough for the moment, and if you are expecting a rigorous analysis of politics, war or various situations that this journalist encountered during the second half of the 20th century in Australia and without, it will not be found in this book. It will, however, feature some curiosities that I have personally found diverting over the years.

I hope you think so too.

1

A WAR WAIF

I was born in 1937, as Adolf Hitler's rush to war was clouding the future of the British Empire, of which Australia was then a loyal card-carrying member. Our Prime Minister Robert Gordon Menzies once famously said we were 'British to the bootstraps'. I missed the Horse's Birthday, 1 August (the date deemed to be the birth day of all horses), coming into this world the following day at Hobart's Queen Alexandra Hospital.

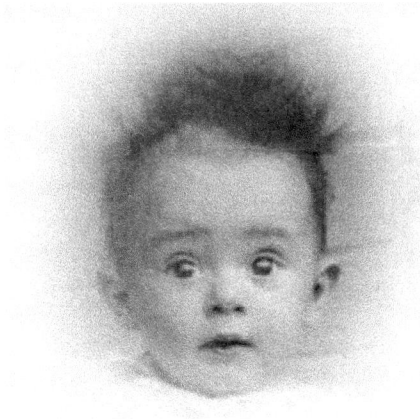

Timothy Gibson Bowden was rather an odd-looking baby at birth, with poppy eyes and hair that made it seem I had been plugged into an electric light socket. Hospitals were draconian institutions in those days, and as my father John Bowden came to pick up his young wife Peggy and newborn son, the matron strode into the reception area to hand me over. My father recalls she behaved 'like a Pommy Sergeant-Major', and in a loud voice for the benefit of all the people in the reception area and nearby corridors, said:

'Now you keep away from that girl for the next three months! You leave her alone.'

My mother, formerly Margaret (Peggy) Lovett, hailed from Launceston in the north of the island state of Tasmania, and my father had been born in the south in Hobart. This meant I had a foot in both camps, as it were, because there was a regional rivalry between the two halves of Tasmania that made the bloody rivalry between the Republic of Ireland and the British-controlled north look like a mild brawl in a primary school playground by comparison. (Well… it was pretty intense anyway.)

The history of how this rivalry came about cannot be dealt with here but it was, and is still, very real.

In 1967, the deadly 'Black Tuesday' bush fires on 7 February, the worst in Tasmania's history, left 62 people dead, 900 injured and over 7000 homeless. The total damage amounted to $40 million dollars in today's values. A Launceston friend of mine swore that he saw a hand-lettered sign in a shop window two weeks after the catastrophe:

WANTED – 350 GOOD MEN AND TRUE
TO MARCH ON THE SOUTH
WHILE THEY ARE STILL WEAK

Ask any Tasmanian, away from his beloved island, where he or she comes from, and they will say 'Tasmania' rather than 'Australia'. Island people believe they have special qualities, denied to lesser mortals.

In later years, when I became a journalist, I attempted to define this, and my effort was actually read into Hansard into the House of Representatives by a colourful Hobart politician, the Liberal member for Franklin Bruce Goodluck, on 25 February 1987. He began:

'I would like to read a little quote from [a] Tasmanian, Tim Bowden from the Australian Broadcasting Corporation, when he launched a book *The Doubleman* which is written by a fellow classmate of mine Christopher Koch. I think that what he said is not rude, it is great.'

MR CAMPBELL: Hurry up!

MR GOODLUCK: The honourable member should be quiet. He stated: Tasmania is the testicle of Australia – suffusing the Mainland with strength and vigour.

What a pity there is only one of them!

TASMANIA – 'THE ISLAND EVER SWEET AND FAIR...'

Many years ago, someone sent me one Skipper Francis' Ode to Tasmania, which I feel compelled to share.

There's a grand and stately island,
Standing in the Tasman Sea.
Where the mountains gird the meadows
And cool winds blow fresh and free.
Hill and dale present a picture,
Silver sand lies around her shores.
Pleasant days I've spent in Tassie,
Hope I'm spared for many more.
CHORUS
Tasmania, Tasmania, your worth has not been told,
For many a glorious sunset
Has covered you in gold.
The heavens send their blessing
In sweet showers of rain.
When I leave I won't be happy
Till I'm back in Tassie again.

13

So who was Skipper Francis? Walter William Francis was born in 1886 and handed in his cheque in 1957. I am not sure where he was born, probably Britain, as one of his accomplishments was to swim the Bristol Channel. He was most noted for encouraging Australians to join up and fight the Hun in World War I by writing patriotic songs – the most famous, FOR AULD LANG SYNE! AUSTRALIA WILL BE THERE.

He certainly must have visited Australia to form such a passionate bond with the Testicle State, but I can't find out if he ever came here to live.

It was pleasing to read that his patriotic songs were 'written, composed and sung with phenomenal success'. There is more, but I think one verse and chorus is plenty...

Peggy (for some reason she refused to be called Mum or Mummy) was soon to be a single parent, as my father enlisted in the AIF in 1939 when war was declared and was soon off to the Middle East in some style on the huge pre-war liner Aquitania. Like most Australians then, few had been abroad. The furthest from Tasmania my father had been in his life was across Bass Strait by ferry to Melbourne. He was then 33 years old.

I had to wait six years before I got to know him. Money was short, and Peg had to work. One of her jobs was as a wartime censor, checking outgoing letters to see no details of Australia of use to an enemy got through. The offending material was simply cut out with scissors.

Money was short and after a year or so she had to move out of the family home that had been built in time for my arrival, and rent it out. For a while we lived with friends in a nearby street, Philip and Peg Waterworth, who had two daughters, the eldest Philippa my age.

In those days groceries were home delivered in wooden boxes packed by grocers in white aprons, and every item wrapped in crisp white paper. My mother ordered what she needed by telephone. One morning she was alone in the Waterworth house and in the loo. The phone was in the hall, mounted quite high on the wall.

I was three, and from the smallest room she heard me lug a chair along to the phone so I could climb up and reach it. She heard me say: 'Peg can't come to the phone at the moment, she's in the lavatory.'

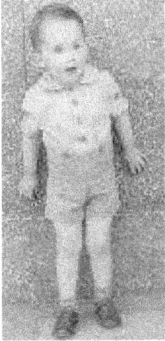

But wait a minute, I think she's about to come out.'

'I can hear the paper rustling, and yes – she's pulled the chain and here she comes!'
My mother presumed it was one of her women friends, but in fact it was the man from man from Beck's Groceries ringing for the weekly order.

As a young boy, a visit to the shoe shop was most exciting. It was the era of the fluoroscope – a wondrous machine that stood on a pedestal, ostensibly to help with shoe fitting. No shoe shop, even in remote Hobart, was without one. There was a viewing portal for the salesman, your mother, and you.

I recall standing in front of it with my new school shoes on, and edging both feet into a slot at the bottom. A button was pressed, and a low whine was heard from the bowels of the contraption. As you gazed into a viewing portal, the bones of your feet were revealed on a green screen and you could wiggle your toes and see the skeletal image move.

You could also see the nails around the edge of the shoe in this X-ray image, and whether there was enough room (or too much) between your feet and the boundaries of the shoe.

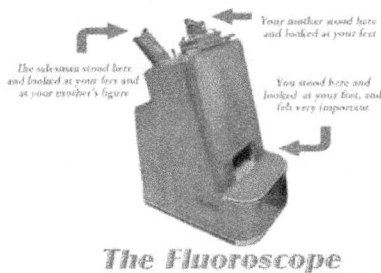

Your mother stood here and looked at your feet

The salesman stood here and looked at your feet and at your mother's figure

You stood here and looked at your feet, and felt very important.

The Fluoroscope

Every shoe shop had one, and busy mothers would order their sons and daughters to 'play' there, while they discussed various options for their own shoes as well as the kids.

This, in hindsight, was unwise as our developing gonads were being subjected to large doses of radiation from the largely unshielded radio-active core of the fluoroscope while we kids marvelled at the spectral images of our feet for sometimes 10 to 15 minutes.

In truth the fluoroscopes were spewing out radiation literally all over the shop, whether they were being used or not. Those having a fitting got the most powerful dose, being closest to the radioactive core. But the hapless staff who worked there were permanently in range and received radiation all the time.

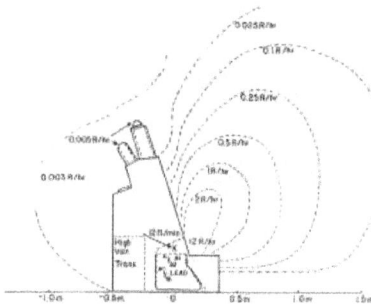

This diagram shows the radiation emitted at varying distances from the fluoroscope. The dose was measured in roentgens per hour.

Believe it or not, the amount of radiation being absorbed by shoe shop staff was not measured until the 1950s!

Even by the 1920s, when these contraptions were first invented, the dangers of radiation were well known, but not by the general public.

As far back at as 1908 the annual meeting of the American Roentgen Association heard a report that 47 people had died due to radiation exposure. Some of these victims were hailed as 'martyrs to science'.

When the fluoroscopes were measured in the 1950s the results were frightening. In addition to the dosage being received by the feet, the entire body of the customer, as well as the salesman and parent, was bathed in radiation. Others waiting in the shop were being irradiated through the walls of the machine. Even in the waiting room, the permissible daily dose of radiation would be received by a single person in an hour! Shoe-store staff (and customers) were at risk of stunted growth, dermatitis, cataracts, malignant cancers and sterility. No focused medical study was EVER done on the effects of these machines.

The truth of the matter was that shoe shop staff (and their bosses) always knew that the fluoroscopes were completely useless as an aid to fitting shoes, but wonderful as a sales gimmick. This ad by Altra shows how bogus the whole thing was. The bones in your feet would never separate in this way, wider shoes or not.

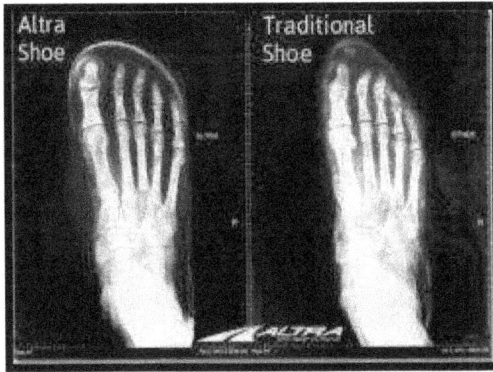

In the United States and Canada legislative action to limit the use of fluoroscopes was slow, but did occur before the end of the 1950s and most had disappeared – but not completely – by the 1970s.

In fact, by the early 1960s, shoe merchants were flogging off their fluoroscopes to whoever was silly enough to buy them for a fraction of their original cost. Some were donated to schools for science classes, others slipped into the attics or basements of private citizens. Would you believe a functioning fluoroscope (still quietly emanating its poisonous radiation) was discovered in the basement of a shoe-shop in Ontario in 1996?

Major John Bowden was discharged from the Australian Army in 1944, and I had a father again. His return was marked by the birth of my brother Nicholas, followed by Philip and lastly (to my parents' great delight) a daughter, Lisa. Nicholas did not arrive till two years after his return. I was seven. My father recalls Peg at first said, 'The desert sands must have burnt you out'. I was seven when my brother Nicholas was brought home from the Queen Alex. hospital. My parents were progressive for their era, and involved me in from an early age with basic accounts of babies growing 'inside Peg's tummy', and breast feeding.

I have been told I could hardly wait for the first feeding session, and asked where Peg was going to sit. I drew up a small stool near the sofa indicated, sat down on it and waited for the action. Peg, a modern mother, sat down, produced a breast and baby Nicholas obligingly began sucking vigorously. Apparently I jumped up from my little seat, and took in this wondrous sight from every angle, including close-ups. After a time, Peg recalled, I said:

'What happens if he blows instead of sucks?'

I am indebted to Merle Jantzen, one of my mother's friends, who unexpectedly emailed me in 2008 about the difficulty of acquainting seven- year-olds with the basic facts of life.

I remember a lunch held in Hobart by Claire Mitchell, where a gaggle of young women (and their kids) were present. The mums were listening indulgently to the children chatting happily just outside the sunroom window. The talk evolved to babies. One knowing little sod – not you this time – said that babies grew inside the mother's tummy. You refused to believe this and got quite angry with the child who had made this claim.

You stormed inside to the group of mums and, stood in front of Peg with your hands on your hips and demanded: 'Is it true that I came out of your stummick'? Peggy, somewhat taken aback and a little embarrassed but determined to follow the modern trend and not push the cabbage-patch bit went a little pink, and said, 'Yes Tim, that is true'.

You glared at her as only a seven-year-old can, stamped your foot, and said: 'Well, I think that is disgusting,' and stormed out.

At this time, our hostess, Claire Mitchell, was heavily pregnant herself. The kid who had first advanced the tummy theory told the other kids there that Claire was about to have a baby.

Asked how you could tell, you volunteered: 'Well she looks as if she is wearing dozens of aprons – that's how!'

At a later social gathering at Claire's house, the topic of tummies and aprons was again discussed by kids outside the sunroom window.

This time you were more offhand about it, and it was you that came in to ask the key question, 'How do the babies get out'?

None of the mums was quite up to explaining the details and after a long pause you turned to your own mother, slapped her on her backside, and said: 'Well I guess that's the obvious place!' Then once again made a dramatic exit.

In 1948 my parents and four of their friends made a brave decision to walk the central Tasmanian mountains track from Lake St Clair to Cradle Mountain, a hike of some 80 kilometres. The really courageous part of this exercise was to take me! I was then 10 years old, and I don't know what their companions thought about the prospect of me going – but I can guess.

Few people went bushwalking in those days. If you met someone else on the single track coming the other way you were disappointed as you felt you had the right to have the wilderness to yourself. In the 21st century thousands of visitors walk the Overland Track, as it is now known, in summer and (unwisely in my opinion) in winter. The boggy buttongrass swamps that we negotiated in our boots and gaiters, mud (sometimes sloshing up to our knees) are now all protected by board walks, and the handful of rough slab huts available along the route have been replaced by a variety of upmarket accommodation, some companies stocking them with fine wines and gourmet food for their customers and arranging for their clients to carry only light day packs for each day of the six stage walk.

Haversacks were primitive with a small metal frame from which the bag, with extra pockets, hung down dragging on your shoulders.

Everything had to be carried in them, emergency tents, food, billycans for open fires (now strictly verboten) and mercifully some high-energy food like raisins and chocolate, which supplemented the dehydrated stews, porridge, milk powder and soup cubes that were available then.

My mother Peg was still getting over the birth of my brother Philip the previous year and really should not have gone, as she hated that kind of thing anyway. My father was an outdoor enthusiast, as were the Waterworth brothers, Phil and David, and their wives Peggy and Betty – although Betty was a total novice at that stage.

We planned to take ten days to do the 50 miles, with some side excursions to high country attractions like a place called the Labyrinth, which was well named because we got lost on to the way to it, rather than in it, and had to retrace our steps to find the overland track again.

We had reached the northern section of the trek, passing Tasmania's highest peak Mt Ossa (1617 metres) named after a mountain in Greek mythology, to be almost in sight of Cradle Mountain, when we stopped for a rest beside the track. To our collective amazement we heard and then saw a young man running towards us complete with pack. He stopped to tell us that a young woman had been bitten by a tiger snake and had collapsed in the Mt Pelion hut. He was trying to get help from the police and a doctor at the nearest town of Sheffield, about another 80 kilometres to the north.

As it happened, we had a doctor in our small party. David Waterworth was a specialist eye surgeon. He did not volunteer that he was a doctor, and no one else said anything. Later, in his defense, David said that judging by the nature of the bite she almost certainly would not have survived the first night, and this sadly turned out to be true when days later a doctor and police did get to her. My father and Phil Waterworth said they would go with him as far as Waldheim, a chalet at the end of the overland track. My father said later the first thing they did was stop him running.

The young woman was the only female in a small group of four, members of a church bushwalking club. She had waited decorously while the men walked on in order to pee. She used a fallen log for support and of all things, urinated on a tiger snake, which reared up and bit her on or near her private parts.

Now every snake in Tasmania is poisonous and the tiger snake is at the top of the list. Tasmanian bushwalkers always wear long trousers and gaiters, as the tiger snake has grooved fangs down which its venom travels to kill its prey. If it bites a human through protective clothing, most of the venom ends up in the clothing.

Even then it can be touch and go. In this situation there was no hope. The young woman was embarrassed about what had happened, and did not tell her male companions of the bizarre nature of her toilet stop until she collapsed on the track.

NOCTURNAL NUDIST AT SANDY BAY

This headline even made it into the news pages of The Hobart *Mercury*.

Our family home at 37 Maning Avenue, Sandy Bay, was built at the top of quite a steep hill. This did give us water glimpses of the Derwent Estuary, but basically our house was difficult to get to because of the hill.

Winters in Hobart could (and can) be extremely cold. One of my earliest memories is being taken outside by my father to see a brilliant display of the *Aurora Australis* which had by some trick of the atmosphere made its way all the way to Hobart from the Antarctic, displaying improbable shimmering curtains of green and red in the night sky, the result of collisions between energetic electrons, atoms and molecules in the upper atmosphere.

In the late 1940s my mother Peg used to meet one of her women friends to go to see a movie in the city. 'Going to the pictures' was the phrase used then.

One evening in mid-winter, she walked up our also steep driveway to the top of Maning Avenue to walk down and meet her friend with whom she would catch a tram along Sandy Bay Road to the picture theatre of their choice. My father stayed at home to mind me.

As she reached the top of the Bowden drive on a frosty night, she was surprised to say the least to see a completely naked man standing in the roadway. I suppose it says something about the comparative innocence of those times that she did not have any sense of alarm. She decided to ignore him and set off down the hill to meet her friend.

The naked man fell into step beside her, and they began to walk silently down the road together. Peg said later that she felt this was ridiculous, and decided that when she got under the next street light and she would look at him to see if she knew him.

No words were spoken until they came under the light. Peg turned to face him (she didn't know him) and said, 'Aren't you cold'?

He muttered, 'Well yes I am a bit', rushed down the hill a bit further into a hedge, pulled on a sweater and trousers and rode off on a bicycle.

My mother thought to herself, 'Well that was odd', and met her friend, who freaked out. 'We must call the police immediately and report this!' This was probably done, because otherwise it would not have made the morning paper.

POSTSCRIPT: Some of her cynical friends put it about that what she had really said was, 'Aren't you cold, dear?'

My mother Peggy hated being photographed, but during the war occasionally used street photographers to be able to have photos of her and first born son (and war orphan) sent to my father John Bowden, then in the Palestine with the AIF.

2

LEARNING TO STEAL OTHERS' WORDS, PHRASES AND STORIES

As English was my best (and most loved) subject at school, I decided I wanted to be a journalist. Jobs were easier to get back in 1956 and I was taken on by *The Mercury* in Hobart as a cadet reporter. It is a decision I have never regretted. Then the paper was produced by a process that dated back to William Caxton, with linotype machines and hot metal, which when cooled was slotted into flat page formats with metal slugs capped with reverse print.

An impression was taken of the flat page with a flexible matrix and bent into a hoop shape which was cast in metal. The following page was treated similarly, and the heavy casts were bolted together on both sides of the cylinders on the huge printing presses. When, in the early morning, the presses rolled, the huge roll of virgin newsprint went through the printing rollers and was cleverly sliced and cut to be compiled into the morning paper. The whole building used to shake when the presses rolled.

Journalists typed their stories on small squares of rough copy paper (for economic reasons the same grade of paper *The Mercury* was printed on).

So what qualities made up a good journalist? Someone sent me a clipping from an unknown magazine which I thought summed it up superbly. I do not know who wrote it, but it deserves a wider airing. The clipping is too hard to read here, but this is what he said:

The only qualities essential for real success in journalism are rat-like cunning, a plausible manner and a little literary ability. The rat-like cunning is needed to ferret out and publish things that people don't want to be known (which is – and always will be – the best definition of news). The plausible manner is useful for surviving while this is going on, helpful with the entertaining presentation of it, and even more useful in later life when the successful journalist may have to become a successful executive on his newspaper. The literary ability is of obvious use.

Other qualities are helpful, but not diagnostic. These include a knack with telephone, trains and petty officials; a good digestion and a steady head, 'total recall'; enough idealism to inspire indignant prose (but not enough to inhibit detached professionalism); a paranoid temperament; an ability to believe passionately in second rate projects; well-placed relatives; good luck; the willingness to betray, if not friends, acquain-tances; a reluctance to understand too much too well; an implacable hatred of spokesmen, administrators, lawyers, public relations men, politicians and all those who would rather pervert words than policies; and the strength of character to lead a disrupted personal life without going completely haywire. And to get a job in journalism you need to be determined and persistent.

Regarding the ability to steal others' words and phrases – that one about rat-like cunning was stolen from a colleague.

....

The Mercury was rated as a national newspaper in a state capital. In reality Hobart was like a big country town, but the training for cadets was excellent. You were apprenticed to the various 'roundsmen' – women only did the social pages then – which included shipping, civic (the Town Hall), state parliament, police (including the courts), sport including foot-ball and horse racing. All reporters had to wear a suit and tie to work whether you were chasing fire engines or covering the Magistrates Court.

The courts were never dull. One magistrate, rejoicing in the name of Hubert Mansel Brettingham-Moore, had a great sense of humour. But on this particular morning in 1956 he was particularly irritated by the number of motorists caught speeding on Sandy Bay Road.

He finally rounded on the tenth defendant so charged and said, 'I've had enough of this, I'm going to make an example of you'.

Reaching under the bench, he produced a black cap, put it on and intoned sonorously, 'It is the sentence of this court that you be taken from here to a prison, and thence to a place of execution, and that there you shall be hanged by the neck until you are dead. And may the Lord have mercy on your soul…'

There was a stunned silence in the traffic court. Then someone jumped up at the back and said, 'You can't do that – you haven't got the authority'!

'Oh, haven't I?' said Brettingham-Moore, taking off his black cap. 'Oh well – fined 10 pounds.'

I was not in court at the time, but the senior police roundsman, Rex Mitchell, was and confirmed the story with me many years later.

Part of a cadet's training was to learn Pitmans shorthand, and we were given weekly lessons by the football roundsman, Keith Welsh. *The Mercury* had a policy of never giving journalists a byline (seems quaint now) and Keith wrote his football coverage under the pseudonym 'Drop Kick'.

Inevitably we cadets called him 'Drip Cock' – but not to his face.

Even in those early days I kept keeping a record of headlines with a double-entendre, and I remember others which have been mislaid, but stuck in my mind. It is time to give them a belated airing.

BENGAL TIGER FOR HOBART CUP

Must have caused a frisson in the stands…

Billy Graham marries his daughter

Really? I never heard about that before…

State marksmen upset by wind

Aren't we all?

ROBBER GETS AWAY WITH £1,235 PAYROLL IN SNATCH

You'd think they might have taken a canvas bag with them…

After the Iranian revolution, the exiled Shah of Persia briefly took his retinue to the Bahamas.

SHAH STICKS IT OUT ON RESORT

Some kind of gesture to the Ayatollahs?

Hobart had a quite successful racehorse named after the well-known Tasmanian apple variety, Granny Smith. The good burghers of Hobart awoke one Saturday morning to see a two-column wide headline on the sporting pages with the following prediction...

GRANNY HAS IT SEWN UP

The mind boggles...

This one is more recent, from the *Great Lakes Advocate*, the local paper where I currently live on the mid north coast of New South Wales. The local dramatic society turned on a Christmas pantomime. But it can't have been this bad, surely?

Great Lakes Advocate

Wednesday January 1 2003

IN BRIEF

Pantomime proves a big shit

Great Lakes Amateur Dramatic Society's latest production, a children's pantomime titled "Red Riding Hood", has been hailed as a great success.

The show will have its final performance at the Forster Tuncurry Memorial Services Club tomorrow at 8pm.

The show, directed by William Sherlock, stars many GLADS members including Helen Duggan, Helen Blakiss, Shirley Craig, Jenny Curtis, Chris Jones and Debbie Prewett, and introduces a delightful number of young actors and dancers from the local region, including Red Riding Hood herself, Freya Meade.

The cast has been rehearsing since September.

This reminds me of a drama critic, commenting on another amateur production who wrote:

'For many of the young players it was a first appearance, and they displayed their parts with dignity and poise'.

But happily not in the Forster Tuncurry Memorial Services Club on this occasion.

My favourite from the 1950s is coverage by *The Mercury* of an outing by Hobart's Catholic Archbishop Guilford Young in 1955. Only 31 years old when he was appointed, he made up for his youthful appearance by adopting a gravitas beyond his years. Always dressed in his Archbishop's black robes, he moved slowly and spoke deliberately in a deep sonorous voice wherever he went, in church and in this case attending a function at the Hobart Town Hall with his visiting two visiting civilian brothers, who could have doubled for plainclothes coppers. This was regrettable due to the headline for an entirely different story which was unfortunately placed directly beneath this photograph on page 3.

SEX MANIAC:
POLICE
WARNING

In 1990 someone sent me this heading from a Hobart suburban give-away, *The Southern Star*. It even boasted a financial section, with the following headline outlining possible good buys for the canny investor in the current difficult financial climate.

Business

If you can't pick the bottom, here's the next best thing

Your nose perhaps?

....

The impermanence and transitory nature of the newspaper story as a historical record was demonstrated to me vividly in 1955, shortly after joining *The Mercury* as a cadet reporter.

Noticing a touring cyclist from Europe pausing on his heavily laden beflagged machine to get his bearings in front of the newspaper office, I asked him some questions, jotted down his answers and dashed inside to inveigle one of the photographers to snap a pic. It all worked out, and I had the great joy the next morning of seeing my first ever published and illustrated story in the paper.

About a week later I happened to visit a hamlet on the rural fringe of Hobart, improbably named Bagdad, to interview a local resident. I needed to use 'the smallest room' which in this case was a traditional weatherboard one-holer out the back. Squares of torn up newspaper on a spike were the sole concession to basic hygiene.

I was a little surprised and at first concerned that my prized story of the beaming Swedish cyclist was hanging there as the first option.

I used it, too. It was at least a variant on the old saw 'today's news wraps tomorrow's fish and chips'. Nor was the irony of the situation lost on this 18-year-old fledgling reporter meditating on his journalistic future in that country dunny.

The Mercury reporters' room was Spartan to say the least – a bit like a big secondary school classroom. A long built in wooden desk fronted the windows overlooking Macquarie Street. It was distinguished by a line of literally hundreds of cigarette burns along its front edge. These occurred when a journalist would come in close to deadline to write his news story.

If he didn't have any cigarettes, he would frantically importune one from a colleague, light it, take one long drag and put it down on the edge of the desk – where it would slowly burn away unattended as the journo banged away at his typewriter.

It had to be his own typewriter too, because *The Mercury* management was too mean to provide them. There were a couple of old chaff-cutters, an Olivetti and Imperial, on two of the separate tables elsewhere in the reporters' room for emergencies, but that was that.

Everybody smoked and drank prodigiously. (For some reason I never took up smoking but like everyone else did not foreswear the demon drink.) In winter, with all the doors and windows shut against the frigid air outside, the whole editorial floor was clouded in a thick haze of blue smoke which everyone breathed – and took for granted.

I recall one of my fellow cadet reporters, John Sorell, was assigned one night to cover the annual meeting of the Hobart Temperance Society. He went down to the pub and got drunk instead and returned to the office dangerously close to deadline. He did have a program giving the basics of the meeting before it happened. Johnsy was so pissed he actually fell sideways off his chair before he started to type. Returning undaunted to the task at hand, he began to make it all up.

'Alcohol continues to be the greatest curse threatening the stability of our society today', said the President of the HTS Mr Eustace Clatworthy. 'Battered women and abused children are the innocent victims of this pernicious habit.' This went on, line after line.

John (who was later the News Editor of Channel Nine in Melbourne for more than 30 years) then fell asleep while someone else submitted his copy. Although all of this was fabricated, no one from the temperance society ever complained. Doubtless Mr Clatworthy was surprised and delighted to get the unexpected publicity.

....

If ever there was role model for journalists not to take themselves too seriously, Claude Cockburn is a superb candidate. Once, while working as a sub-editor on the august *The Times* of London, he got away with a single column heading of wondrous insignificance:

SMALL EARTHQUAKE
IN CHILE
NOT MANY HURT

Like many a good communist, Cockburn was born in 1904 with a silver spoon in his mouth. He survived a splendidly eccentric English childhood, rather reminiscent of Nancy Mitford's world. After a public school and Oxford (he edited the university magazine *ISIS* for a time) he won a travelling scholarship. This was fortuitous, as he had been living beyond his means and needed the money to pay off his creditors. There was enough money to get to Berlin, where he contributed an occasional piece to *The Times* through its resident correspondent there.

By being in the right spot at the right time he managed to bypass the entire journalistic training system and was invited back to Printing House Square by the legendary (later pro-Nazi) editor Geoffrey Dawson.

He later wrote this wonderful description of life in the Foreign Editorial Room of *The Times*.

A sub-editor was translating a passage of Plato's *Phaedo* for a bet. Another sub-editor had declared it could not be done without losing a certain nuance of the original. He was dictating the Greek passage aloud from memory.

That very first evening I saw the chief sub-editor hand a man a slip of Reuters' Agency tape with two lines on it, saying that the Duke of Gloucester had arrived at Kuala Lumpur and held a reception. It would run to about half-an-inch. I dare say it could have been got ready for the printer in a matter of minutes. I was glad to see nothing of that kind happened here.

The sub-editor, a red-bearded man with blazing blue eyes who looked like a cross between John the Baptist and Captain Kettle, had at the age of 20 or thereabouts written the definitive grammar of an obscure Polynesian language and gone on to be – a curious position for an Englishman – a professor of Chinese metaphysics in the University of Tokyo. He took the two-line slip of paper into the library, and then to the Athenaeum Club, where he sometimes used to go for a cold snack during *The Times* dinner hour.

His work was completed only just in time for the 10 o'clock edition. It had been a tricky job. 'There are', he explained, '11 different ways of spelling Kuala Lumpur, and it's difficult to decide which should, as it were, receive the imprimatur of *The Times*.'

Cockburn very quickly won the job of *The Times* Washington correspondent. The handover from the incumbent was brief to say the least

– but time for the departing reporter to give Cockburn the two best bits of journalist advice he ever received. It was the financial crash year of 1929.

'I think it well', he said, 'to remember that when writing for the newspapers we are writing for an elderly lady in Hastings who has two cats of which she is passionately fond. Unless our stuff can compete for her interest with those cats, it is no good.'

The second, shouted from the window of his already moving taxi, 'Remember old boy, whatever happens, you are right and London is wrong.

My favourite of all Cockburn's pertinent quotes on journalism is: 'Never believe anything until it is officially denied.'

....

I am sure Claude Cockburn would have enjoyed the following headlines, gleefully collected by Gordon Balfour Haynes, of the *Echo* ('grammar nazi'):

INCLUDE YOUR CHILDREN WHEN BAKING COOKIES
SOMETHING WENT WRONG IN JET CRASH, EXPERTS SAY
POLICE BEGIN CAMPAIGN TO RUN DOWN JAYWALKERS
IRAQI HEAD SEEKS ARMS

IS THERE A RING OF DEBRIS AROUND URANUS?

PROSTITUTES APPEAL TO POPE

PANDA MATING FAILS; VETERINARIAN TAKES OVER
TEACHER STRIKES IDLE KIDS

CLINTON WINS BUDGET; MORE LIES AHEAD

PLANE TOO CLOSE TO GROUND, CRASH PROBE TOLD
MINERS REFUSE TO WORK AFTER DEATH

JUVENILE COURT TO TRY SHOOTING DEFENDANT
STOLEN PAINTING FOUND BY TREE

WAR DIMS HOPE FOR PEACE

IF STRIKE ISN'T SETTLED QUICKLY, IT MAY LAST A WHILE
COUPLE SLAIN; POLICE SUSPECT HOMICIDE

KIDS MAKE NUTRITIOUS SNACKS

LOCAL HIGH SCHOOL DROPOUTS CUT IN HALF
TYPHOON RIPS THROUGH CEMETERY; HUNDREDS DEAD
SCHOOLBOYS GET FIRST HAND JOB EXPERIENCE

MINISTER LAUNCHES PROBE INTO CONTRACEPTIVE
POLICE STONED

CHILD'S   STOOL   MAKES   INTERESTING
GARDEN ORNAMENT

FERTILE WOMAN DIES NEAR CLIMAX: headline in a North
Dakota newspaper (Climax being a town there)

....

The Mercury in my time was a broadsheet paper, as were many other
metropolitan dailies, including The Melbourne *Herald* and *The Age*, and
the Brisbane *Courier Mail* just to name a few. But by the 21st century,
with the competition of the digital era and falling circulations, tabloids
are the fashion and they are getting more anorexic by the week. Only
Rupert Murdoch's *The Australian* is a broadsheet, and that may be because
Murdoch is rich enough to subsidise it for old time's sake. Michael Leunig
summed up the dilemma as only he can.

The demise of the broadsheet
newspaper is a terrible tragedy mate,
especially to those of us who appreciate
its civilizing influence on a cold frosty night

....

In the late 20th century, the now defunct British humorous magazine *Punch* celebrated its 150th year of publication, and included some odd and unusual examples of journalism culled from many countries and a variety of periodicals and newspapers. Australia got a mention.

Errol Flynn 'a Hollywood tragedian of Tasmanian origin' is noted for his amorous reputation. And for playing *You Are My Sunshine* on the pianoforte - without the use of his hands.

The magazine comments: 'It is not known whether he enjoyed any success with his unconventional approach to the instrument [the pianoforte that is] but, as Dr Johnson said of a dog walking on hind legs, "It is not a question of it being done well but that one is surprised to find it done at all".'

From the *Worthing Guardian* came: 'The steamy film *Nine-And-A-Half Weeks* has been temporarily banned from Worthing's Dome Cinema until it has been privately viewed by Worthing Council's moral watchdogs. The film *Body Lust – Best Bit Of Crumpet In Denmark* will be shown instead.'

The Trinidad Guardian featured with: 'LOST – Bull Terrier, has three legs, blind in left eye, missing right ear, broken tail, recently castrated. Answers to the name of Lucky.'

It is easy to make mistakes, as the *Dalhousie Gazette* recognised: 'Gerald Harris, whose name was incorrectly given as Harold Morris and who is 39 and not 93 as stated in the story, is an associate professor of Tort Law School and not a janitor at the public library as the story incorrectly stated.'

This one is from *The Sun-Herald* in Sydney. 'A public notice in the classified ads section recently read: "I, Satpaul Dikshit, of Harris Park, will henceforth write my name as Satpaul Dixit". And who could blame him?'

....

RANGING FURTHER AFIELD

'Irish police are being handicapped in a search for a stolen van, because they cannot issue a description. It's a special branch vehicle and they don't want the public to know what it looks like.' (*The Guardian*)

'After being charged £20 for a £10 overdraft, 30-year-old Michael Howard of Leeds changed his name by deed poll to Yorkshire Bank PLC Are Fascist Bastards. The bank has now asked him to close his account, and Mr. Bastards has asked them to repay the 69 pence balance, by cheque, made out in his new name.'(*The Guardian*)

'Would the congregation please note that the bowl at the back of the church labelled "for the sick" is for monetary donations only.' (*Church-town Parish Magazine*)

'There must, for instance, be something very strange in a man who, if left alone in a room with a tea-cosy, doesn't try it on.' (*Glasgow Evening News*)

'A young girl who was blown out to sea on a set of inflatable teeth was rescued by a man on an inflatable lobster. A coastguard spokesman commented, "This sort of thing is all too common".' (*The Times*)

'At the height of the gale, the harbourmaster radioed a coastguard on the spot and asked him to estimate the wind speed. He replied that he was sorry, but he didn't have a gauge. However, if it was any help, the wind had just blown his Land Rover off the cliff.' (*Aberdeen Evening Express*)

'Mrs Irene Graham of Thorpe Avenue, Boscombe, delighted the audience with her reminiscence of the German prisoner of war who was sent each week to do her garden. He was repatriated at the end of 1945. She recalled: "He'd always seemed a nice friendly chap, but when the crocuses came up in the middle of our lawn in February 1946, they spelt out HEIL HITLER".' (*Bournemouth Evening Echo*)

'Commenting on a complaint from a Mr. Arthur Purdey about a large gas bill, a spokesman for North West Gas said "We agree it was rather high for the time of year. It's possible Mr. Purdey has been charged

for the gas used up during the explosion that blew his house to pieces".'
(*Northern Post*)

....

One of the most important parts of a young journalist's training is how to fiddle expenses to augment the lousy pay. This has to be done creatively - but without overkill. But sometimes creativity has to be defended. I worked in South East Asia for the ABC in the mid-sixties, and got to know Neil Davis very well. He covered front-line combat in the Indo China war for an amazing 11 years, and was sadly killed in Bangkok in 1985 covering an attempted *coup d'etat* there.

This story goes back to his first year in Asia in 1964, when he was sent to Kuching in East Malaysia on assignment and put in his expenses when he got back to the ABC office in Singapore. His boss there at the time was a noted character and legendary drunk, Ted Shaw, who outdid Walter Mitty in inventing exploits that never happened. Ted claimed in his cups to have broken wild brumbies in Queensland, played test cricket for Australia, and interviewed Hitler in the Berchtesgaden before the war – all at the same time. Ted was a great story teller over a beer, but he wasn't much of an administrator, as he was too lazy to bother about all the detail. But he had learned the old supervisor's trick of glancing over expense receipts and homing in on a dodgy one. Neil Davis, unlike most journalists, was meticulously scrupulous about not gilding the lily on expenses, but with this receipt he'd slipped up. The dance halls and bars in South East Asia those days had what were called taxi dancers that you hired by the hour. What happened later was another matter. Well Neil had a receipt for his Chinese taxi dancer whose name was Rosette.

Back at the Singapore office Ted, looked suspiciously at Neil. 'What's this bloody Rosette business?'

Now it should be said that Ted was never wrong, and knew everything. Neil had a flash of inspiration. 'You know Ted, the French wine, rosette?'

Ted glared at him: 'Well, why didn't you get Algerian – it's cheaper'.

Mind you, some people never learn. I came across the following memo from a news editor to a newspaper reporter who had been assigned to cover the tall ships leaving Sydney in 1988 during the Bicentenary celebrations.

I note from your expenses claim that you have invoiced us for the hire of a large motor cruiser used to cover the sail-past of the tall ships.

On the live television coverage of this event, you were clearly visible in a small rowing boat.

MEMO TO NEWS EDITOR

Thank you for refreshing my memory. I enclose an additional bill for the cost of hiring the rowing boat used to reach our motor cruiser.

Not be neglected is this expense story concerning the legendary foreign correspondent Rene Cutforth, who joined the BBC in 1946. He became well known as a broadcaster and travelled the world as a BBC correspondent.

He also reported on the Korean War. Reviewing one of his television programs, *The Forties Revisited*, the critic Clive James wrote in *The Observer*, 'Cutforth is that rare thing, a front man with background. Fitzrovia and Soho weigh heavily on his eyelids. His voice sounds like tea-chests full of books being shifted about.'

Cutforth used to be the resident correspondent in Beirut for the BBC in the 1950s. He used to make up his monthly expenses by taking an imaginary spook to lunch. 'Took Carruthers of MI 6 to lunch – eight pounds seven and sixpence' – modest enough sums, but which built up over time. This got up the nose of one of the BBC's accountants who happened to have some intelligence connections. He rang up someone he knew in MI 6 and said, 'I know you can't tell me anything officially old boy, but if you DIDN'T have an operative called Carruthers operating out of Beirut I'd like to know for the following reasons'. His contact said, 'Of course I can't tell you anything officially but…'

Cutforth received a cable to the effect that as MI 6 had never had anyone called Carruthers on their payroll in Beirut, add would he please refund his entertainment claims of the last three years on Carruthers, amounting to the grand total of 257 pounds 10 and sixpence.

Cutforth cabled back instantly: *APPALLED DISCOVER CARRUTHERS AN IMPOSTER STOP I SHALL NOT ENTERTAIN HIM AGAIN STOP CUTFORTH*

....

Cutforth was one of a breed of journalists that is now extinct - the feature reporter who covered the world in the post war - the 50s and 60s. And I mean the whole world. Wherever there was a good breaking story, the great Fleet Street figures like Noel Barbour, Arthur Cooke, Rene McColl, Donald Wise and their ilk would be there, ready to scoop each other. The greatest rivalry of all was between the *Daily Mail* and the *Daily Express*. The *Express* was owned by Lord Beaverbrook, who wouldn't even allow the word 'exclusive' to appear on a story. 'Everything in the *Express* should be exclusive', growled the Beaver.

Today, there are specialist correspondents in most major centres. There is no need for the Great Foreign Correspondent to descend from afar – but it was not always thus.

In 1959 the Dalai Lama decided to go into exile in India following the Chinese take-over of Tibet. For some weeks the world waited for news, as his tiny caravan made its way through the Himalayas towards India. The press arrived in force at a remote region on the Indian border near Nepal where it was thought he might appear. There was absolutely nothing to report, of course, until the Dalai Lama appeared. The 40 or so correspondents banded together to charter a plane to try and over-fly the escaping Tibetans – a pool effort so they could all write 'Today I flew over the Dalai Lama' stories, AND keep an eye on each other at the same time. The press corps arrived at the airfield at the appointed hour, to be told by an apologetic Indian pilot that permission for the flight had been refused.

Noel Barbour of the *Daily Mail* turned to his colleagues in some embarrassment and said: 'Gentlemen I feel it only fair to tell you I filed my story three hours ago'!

When the Dalai Lama did appear, there was enormous pressure on the news agencies to get pictures out. In those days black and white photographs had to be transmitted dot by dot by special machinery only available in major post offices. The head of United Press International, a flamboyant American, Ernie Hoybrecht, had chartered a plane to fly the first photos of the Dalai Lama from the remote border area to the nearest Indian post office able to transmit pictures. So had the rival agency Associated Press, but Ernie was a step ahead. He had a special dark room built in the plane, processed the film in flight, and dashed to the telegraph office at least 15 minutes ahead of AP while 20 shots were transmitted, a process that took about three minutes per photo.

Ernie was lounging against the counter beaming beatifically when the rival AP rep dashed in. As he savoured the moment and his world exclusive, a telegraph clerk came to the counter and said: 'Mr Hoybrecht, here is an urgent flash from your head office. It says: How come your Dalai Lama has beard?'

In the heat of the moment on the border, the UPI photographer had photographed the wrong man! It was the turn of the AP rep to beam and lounge on the counter, knowing that his pix were now first around the world.

This eagerness to be first nearly finished the career of the Daily Express's Arthur Cooke, who was still covering the world in the 1960s. I met him in Singapore during the Vietnam war era. He was working for the *Daily Mail* then, probably as a result of the events that took place in Iran in 1952. The powerful then Prime Minister of Iran, Mohammed Mossadegh, over-threw the Shah over a dispute on oil policy. But the Shah struck back, and returned to power a few days later. Mossadegh was tried for treason, and convicted. The penalty for treason was death by hanging, and Arthur filed his story reporting the trial and that Mossadegh would hang the following morning.

The trouble was Arthur had not fully understood the Iranian system of justice, which was based on the French model. Mossadegh had been found guilty in a committal hearing; the real trial was yet to come. An increasingly distraught Arthur received a cable from his foreign editor Charles Foley asking ominously:

WHY YOUR EXCLUSIVE STILL EXCLUSIVE?

Followed 24 hours later by another:

IT'S MOSSADEGH'S NECK OR YOURS

Mossadegh died of old age in his bed many years later and Arthur switched from the *Daily Express* to the *Daily Mail*.

....

There are many stories told of the *Daily Express'* foreign editor Charles Foley as he attempted to get value for money out of his far flung correspondents. Most of them were not unfond of a drink, and one had been sent to Cairo on an unusually vague assignment. The correspondent propped up the bar at Shepheard's Hotel and had not filed for a week.

Foley cabled him: WHY UNNEWS QUERY FOLEY?

(It was common practice to run words together in cables to save money.)

The Cairo correspondent ordered another drink and reached for a message pad, which the well-trained waiters immediately filed for him.

UNNEWS IS GOOD NEWS.

Within an hour, an urgent cable boomeranged from London.

UNNEWS UNJOB STOP FOLEY

Cairo seems to have been a hazardous assignment on the job front. Another correspondent on assignment there for the *Daily Express* for some months had a girl-friend in Beirut – then famous as the Paris of the Middle East – and used to slip off to see her every weekend. Unfortunately for him the Egyptian army chose a Sunday to overthrow King Farouk. Foley knew where he was though, and an ominous rocket arrived from London.

FAROUK ABDICATED, cabled Foley, WHAT YOUR PLANS?

....

One cannot hope to bribe or twist, Thank God, the British journalist. But seeing what the man will do Unbribed, there's no occasion to.

....

I've been trying, in an eclectic kind of way, to give some insights into the world of journalism – and I began by attempting a definition.

Here are a few more. How I wonder how we might define a columnist?

Someone whose drinking habits no longer allow him or her to meet the public.

A cadet journalist?

A trainee on the same level as a bandage washer in a leper colony.

A public relations executive? (PR people are always executives.)

Public relations is an industry invented so that people in advertising could finally have someone to look down on.

Television reporters shall not escape. This one is from the United States.

Television shows us reporters with $60 haircuts on $6 heads trying to get through four sentences without fluffing.

But I think the status of the journalist in society can be located more precisely following remarks made by the author Dymphna Cusack on ABC Radio, in 1981.

I was accustomed to England where the contempt for writers is quite an established thing. When I wanted an account at Barkers' department store and said I was a writer, they said I would need TWO references, and what was my husband? I said he was a journalist.

They said, 'Then you'll need THREE.'

I have been, unashamedly, a journalist by profession, but surely no-one lived more disgracefully than Jeffrey Barnard, bibulous chronicler of his 'Low Life' column in *The Spectator*. He had always been a heavy drinker, and began in journalism writing a weekly column for *Sporting Life* in 1971, but was sacked in the same year for his uncontrolled drinking.

This precipitated a disastrous period in his life. His third wife left with their two-year-old daughter and he was hospitalised in a detox clinic where he was forced to attend Alcoholics Anonymous sessions. He afterwards always wrote scathingly about AA. After being told by a doctor that he would die very shortly if he continued drinking, he stopped and was 'dry' for almost two years, during which he perhaps unwisely worked as a barman.

He was afterwards to describe this as the worst period of his life and resumed drinking on the grounds that life, if it required sobriety, wasn't worth having. He did change from whisky to vodka to lessen the effects of hangovers.

Barnard continued to submit writing to various papers. He became Racing Correspondent for the satirical magazine *Private Eye*, and even had work accepted by his ex-employer *Sporting Life*. He was given a column in *The Spectator* in 1975. His column, entitled *Low Life* was a contrast to the paper's *High Life* column which described the lives led by wealthy socialites who had luxury yachts, visited casinos and grand hotels.

Instead, Barnard's weekly column chronicled his daily rounds of intoxication and dissipation in the Coach and Horses public house, described by food writer and film maker Jonathan Meades as a 'suicide note in weekly instalments'. Quite often he was too wasted to write his column, and *The Spectator* evolved the policy on these occasions printing a blank space where his column should have been, with the brief comment: 'Jeffery Barnard is unwell' – which his readers knew was code for him being too pissed to meet his deadline.

Not wishing to leave his obituary to some unworthy scribbler, he decided to write his own shortly before he drank himself to death in 1997. In it, he included this description of his early life.

'His drinking began to escalate to such an extent that he was unable to hold down the most ordinary job and he was consequently advised to take up… journalism.'

Oh dear.

3

SCREAMBLED EGGS AND FRIED CRABS BALLS

I was posted to South East Asia in the mid-1960s for the ABC and being an ex-newspaperman, I used to keep a close eye on the English language press. *The Straits Times* in Singapore then used to run a kind of 'man bites dog' spot in the centre of its front page with the standard headline, *JUST FANCY THAT.* I shared a flat with a Reuters correspondent when I first got to Singapore, and he choked on his cornflakes one morning while reading *The Straits Times*. The story (attributed correctly to Reuters) concerned a resident in one of Singapore's high rise buildings who found the lift door open, but no lift. As he stuck his head in to see where the lift was, it promptly shot past and decapitated him. The heading? *JUST FANCY THAT!*

Overseas restaurant menus are often a rich source of misunderstanding. One Asian restaurant in Malaysia once offered me a rather alarming SCREAMBLED EGGS for breakfast. This establishment also had a most unusual and one would presume – fairly rare delicacy, FRIED CRABS BALLS. You'd need a lot of crabs to keep that one served up on a daily basis.

The 1980s and 1990s years I presented a twice weekly television program for the ABC titled BackChat, which gave ABC viewers and listeners an outlet to say what they liked and didn't like about the ABC's output. On one occasion, I asked viewers to send in examples of 'unusual' dishes they may have encountered in Asia.

The response was joyous and immediate. Robin McConville, of Botany, New South Wales, swears he found the following delicacy on the menu of the Sheraton Hotel in Taipei – STEAMED WHOLE CRAP. Only a carping critic would query that one, surely.

Anne Fisher, of Baldry, New South Wales sent in a menu souvenired from a recent overseas trip featuring such delicacies as CRAZY SPICY JELLYFISH, SWEET AND SOUR PIGS HANDS AND FEET, FRIED SNAKEHEAD MULLET BALLS, FRIED GOOSE'S INTESTINES WITH

SALTED VEGETABLE, washed down if so desired with WHITE FUNGUS WITH SUGAR CANDY.

But Romola Shallcross, of Cottesloe, Western Autralia topped that with a dish she found on a Turkish menu – WOMEN'S THIGH BALLS.

Things went from bad to worse. I was forced to reveal some of the gastronomic highlights of Valda and John Lambert's excursion to Thailand. DEEP FAT FRIED PIGS STOMUCH was for breakfast, presumably, after a heavy night.

Looking further afield, Joan Powling, of Ivanhoe, Victoria reported finding the following at a tiny taverna in Crete:

GRILLED LAMP SHOPS, BOWELS TOMATO SPECIAL, and SPLEEN

OMELETTE, WELL COOKED. It would need to be, wouldn't it? Joan said she was gutless enough to give the BOWELS TOMATO SPECIAL a miss, but the GRILLED LAMP SHOPS were delicious.

Today the internet abounds with unfortunate computer translations of both Jinglish and Chinglish signs. I cannot resist passing on this one, which was designed to direct foreign male tourists to a disabled toilet.

残疾人厕所
DEFORMED MAN TOILET

Well. we know what they meant to say…

····

TOILET HAZARDS IN FOREIGN PARTS

I travelled to Japan for the first time in my life in 1983, and spent three weeks in Tokyo, also visiting Kyoto, Hiroshima and Kurashiki City which I reached by the *shinkansen* Japan's famous bullet train which hurtles through the countryside at 300 kilometres per hour. In my work as a journalist I have been lucky enough to visit many Asian countries, but none

was so completely foreign, in my experience, as Japan. I loved the food, of course, although pickled fish for breakfast did not become a permanent habit.

Walking the streets of Tokyo is to see nary a non-Japanese face, and little English is spoken. People are universally friendly to foreigners, although through embarrassment often avoid making eye contact with you if you need to ask directions in the street. If eye contact IS made, they are culturally obliged at least to try and help you rather than walking past.

Before I left Australia I thought it wise to look up some dos and don'ts while in Japan. Their tourist organisation does have English language advice information for first visitors. One of the biggest cultural shocks to the new- comer are Japanese toilets, and that is given particular attention in the briefing. It was valuable information!

Aim Carefully, Please

47

The chances are that sometime during your stay in Japan will find yourself having to use a Japanese-style lavatory. It is not made for sitting down, but don't despair. The receptacle is usually on a raised floor. The opening is rectangular with a sort of hood over one end.

Climb up on the raised floor and stand flat-footed astride the opening with your face towards the hood stop then bend down into a crouching or squatting position, making sure that your rear is over the opening and not protruding beyond it.

The position may not be comfortable but it is sanitary because no part of your body comes in contact with the fixings. In the case of the male, he urinates by standing on the lower floor and aiming for the opening. Please aim carefully!

The most commonly heard word for toilet is *oti-arai*. To ask for the washroom, simply say *toire doko*? [Toilet, where?]

The word for a toilet that is easiest to remember is *benjo*. However, priggish Japanese women object to this word just like some Western women avoid the word 'toilet'.

Public latrines are few and far between – and most of them are filthy. If nature calls when you are out in the streets, the best thing to do to go into the nearest coffee shop or tearoom and invest in the cheapest drink. It won't cost you much more than the tip you have to give to the lavatory attendant in many other countries.

Um, er, and for record I did aim carefully…

....

THIS TOILET SIGN WAS HOME GROWN

Somewhere in the Gulf of North Queensland, I photographed this puzzling instruction in a restaurant loo.

No Foreign Objects
TO BE PLACED IN TOILET BOWLS

"PLEASE USE RECIPROCALS PROVIDED"

....

MANAGEMENT SPEAK

We must not ignore home-grown mangling of the English language, even in the halls of academe. I refer to the perils of management jargon which continues to infest the culture of not only the corporate world but also the universities as well!

The 1990s bred a mania for downsizing, that is, getting rid of anyone who had been around the place longer than five years, thus taking a terrible toll of middle managers over the age of 45 who actually had some corporate memory. This culture was encapsulated in the person of the appalling American business executive Albert 'Chainsaw' Dunlap, who not only ripped through the staff of any company he was associated with, but gave advice to other corporate high flyers on how to sack people and feel good about it. It turned out in the end the feared 'Chainsaw' was a fraudster with psychopathic tendencies.

The big wheel turns, of course, and I was delighted to hear that Dunlap himself was given the flick in the end by the Sunbeam Corporation in 1997 and had to pay them $15 million in damages for his fraudulent business practices. Not long afterwards the corporate culture swung from sacking people to acknowledging that people had become important again and managers were charged with nurturing the staff they once looked to prune. This was coupled with the startling realisation that older staff have a good deal of expertise and wisdom that can actually benefit the company they work for.

The 1980s saw the worst of the psychobabble of corporate navel gazing. Even my own organisation, the ABC was infected with it, although the production of programs composed of thoughts and ideas could hardly be equated with the manufacture of widgets, and judged accordingly. It was the word 'priorisation' which finally snapped my self control and sent me into rug-chewing mode. It seemed to sum up the worst of all the omnipresent management speak that began to blight our working lives.

Even in the ABC we found ourselves struggling in a web of 'mission statements', 'hierarchy of objectives', 'random unilateral impacts', 'action planning', 'world best practice', all leading to the creation of the unstoppable 'corporate plan'.

' Priorisation of objectives' is the phrase which resonated most with me in those desperate days. 'Priorisation' did not appear in any dictionary I could find. It was a bestial assault on the English language, but is unlikely to cause a nanosecond's dismay to those who organised the latest trendy blueprint for corporate spring cleaning.

I could not resist keeping this classic comment from the ABC's Organisation & Methods Department, when one shiny-bummed bureaucrat refused to sanction a payment to a program researcher who was working extra hours for no pay to get the job done. His response was:

'While conscientiousness is praiseworthy and is to be encouraged – it is not something that should be a liability for the ABC.'

I put this in the same class as a program producer when facing managerial obstruction on a particular television documentary blew his top with the admin guy he was dealing with, and said, 'I think you should realise that the ABC actually exists to make programs for radio and television, and that your job is to facilitate this – not make it more difficult'.

His reply? 'I think that is a very narrow-minded attitude to take...'

Now let's consider the dreadful Mission Statement. To the best of my understanding this sets out aims and objectives for the coming year for you or your department if you run one. Then at the end of the year, you are reviewed (doubtless in conjunction with the massively unreadable Corporate Plan). If you haven't achieved the stated aims of the Mission Statement you are presumably given a dreadful bollicking, put on notice to do better or fired. Perhaps I should say 'made excess to requirements'.

The trouble is, the chance that the manager who goaded you into writing your Mission Statement will still be there at the end of that year is remote. Depend on it – there will be a new, ambitious boss just drooling to get his or her hands on the latest shiny levers of the management efficiency systems.

Your original Mission Statement will have as much appeal or interest to your new manager as a dog might evince to a plate of lettuce.

So you start another one, at the same time re-organising your section which has now been incorporated into a different department while you have been trying to rationalise the previous move engineered by the bright spark who triggered your original Mission Statement.

Not all the corporate stuff transposes well into the public service or the universities. An historian friend told me that his humanities faculty had to stop teaching, not so long ago, to work on their Mission Statement for the next financial year. Someone in the history department came up with the bright idea of having 'the pursuit of truth' as one of the nominated goals.

Not a bad concept for a history department, you might think. But the experts in charge of the process said that the pursuit of truth didn't fit the criteria and so they couldn't have it. And why not? asked the baffled historians. Well, we can't quantify it accurately, the management gurus said. It couldn't be quantified or calibrated to make sure that achievable targets were reached.

My friend discussed this with his colleagues and decided to hold out for the pursuit of truth. He found the whole thing distinctly Monty Pythonesque – that the processes of review were actually setting the agendas of the client organisations.

'Philosophy is stuffed for starters', he said to a colleague. 'Clearly the only way we can hold on to the pursuit of truth is to tell lies. We could say that this year we achieved 94.3 per cent, absolute truth, and next year we are confident we can rock in at 95.7 per cent.

I don't think truth made it into the Mission Statement.

No job – even in the public service – is for life any more. And perhaps that's not a bad thing. But how do you locate those who are not pulling their weight? The management consultants have procedures, of course. I once sighted an internal university document which addressed this particular concern. The report stressed the need to identify, and I quote, 'The inadequate performer'.

After having winkled out 'the inadequate performer' the report strongly urged the heads of departments, heads of research schools and the Vice Chancellor 'to act with firm resolve in dealing with these cases'. And we can all guess what that euphemism really meant. 'Here's the door'.

If the identification of the 'inadequate performer' is straightforward enough, the next category is designed to put a chill into the hearts of any yet to be assessed lecturers or tutors. 'How to identify 'The *barely* adequate performer....'

The immediate future

It will be apparent that adoption of proposals 5.1 and 5.2 in relation to future contracts would not begin to alleviate the problems outlined in section 4 until some time in the next decade. In relation to existing contracts, the following observations and suggestions are made:

1) The inadequate performer. It is the Committee's view that adoption of the Board's recommendation concerning the review of the performance of individual academics will provide appropriate documentation on which the University may act to terminate the appointment of the inadequate performer under existing contractual arrangements. It strongly urges heads of departments, heads of research Schools and the Vice-Chancellor to act with firm resolve in dealing with these cases.

2) The barely adequate performer. Again, reviews of performance of individual academics will assist in locating such staff. It is the Committee's view that heads of department within each School should be required to report in writing to the head of the School periodically stating (a) whether, in the opinion of the head of department, any of the tenured academics within his department fall within the "barely adequate performer" category, and if so, (b) what measures have been taken or might be taken to respond to the situation. The heads of Schools should be similarly required to report in writing to the Vice-Chancellor periodically stating (a) whether, in the opinion of the head of School, any of the tenured academics within his School fall within the "barely adequate performer" category, and if so, (b) what measures have been taken or might be taken.

WE TRAINED HARD ..... BUT IT SEEMED THAT EVERYTIME WE WERE BEGINNING TO FORM UP INTO TEAMS WE WOULD BE REORGANISED. I WAS TO LEARN LATER IN LIFE THAT WE TEND TO MEET ANY NEW SITUATION BY REORGANISING; AND A WONDERFUL METHOD IT CAN BE FOR CREATING THE ILLUSION OF PROGRESS, WHILE PRODUCING CONFUSION, INEFFICIENCY AND DEMORALIZATION.

PETRONIUS ARBITER, 210B.C.

Time to upgrade the hierarchy of objectives, wouldn't you say? And the game goes on well into the 21st century. I shall leave the last word to the author of Satyricon, Petronius Arbiter, in 210 BC.

.....

'The future seems to be nothing more than an expensive sequence of never-ending upgrades.' (Mark Trevorrow)

Meanwhile even chief executives are tapping away on their keyboards when once they would have dictated their correspondence to their secretaries or a stenographer (now a vanished breed).

We are all slaves to our computers. Young people are especially afflicted, stabbing obsessively away at their mobile phones or tablets, in the street, on public transport, or anywhere, permanently stressed that they may have not caught up with a Tweet or Facebook message in the last 10 seconds.

But all ages are at it. In Myanmar, of all places, my wife and I were in a restaurant with a Chinese family of four at a nearby table. The children, a boy of about 13 and a girl of 11, were both playing games on their screens. The parents were on their tablets. I don't think anyone exchanged a word during lunch.

In Japan they have replaced the impersonal and unhelpful Microsoft error messages with Haiku poetry verses. Haiku has strict rules. Each poem has only 17 syllables. Five syllables in the first line, seven in the second and five in the third. They are used to communicate timeless messages, often achieving a wistful, yearning and powerful insights through extreme brevity.

Yesterday it worked
Today it is not working
Windows is like that.

The web site you seek
Cannot be located, but
Countless more exist.

Chaos reigns within
Reflect, repent and reboot
Order shall return.

Program aborting
Close all that you have worked on
You ask far too much

Windows NT crashed.
I am the Blue Screen of Death.
No one hears your screams.

Your file was too big.
It must have been quite useful.
But now it is gone.

Stay the patient course.
Of little worth is your ire.
The network is down.

A crash reduces
Your expensive computer
To a simple stone.

Three things are certain:
Death, taxes and lost data.
Guess which has occurred.

You step in the stream,
But the water has moved on.
This page is not here.

Out of memory.
We wish to hold the whole sky.
But we never will.

Having been erased,
The document you are seeking
Must now be retyped.

Serious error.
All shortcuts have disappeared.
Screen. Mind. All is blank.

....

And lastly:

THE CENTIPEDE

The centipede was happy quite,
Until a toad in fun
Said: 'Pray which leg goes after which'?
That worked her mind to such a pitch
She lay distracted in a ditch,
Considering how to run.
(Credited to Mrs Edward Craster, Pinafore Poems 1871)

....

4

SHUFFLING OFF THE MORTAL COIL

As I am now a fledgling octogenarian, the road ahead seems somewhat shorter than it has been. The following verse that I sent to my father John Bowden when he was 85 now seems more relevant.

GROWING OLD

Just a line to say I'm living,
That I'm not in bed or dead.
Though I'm getting more forgetful
And more mixed up in the head.

At times I don't remember,
When standing at the stair
If I must go up for something,
Or have I just been there?

And before the fridge so often
My mind is filled with doubt.
Have I just put food away;
Or have I come to take it out?

And there are times when it is dark
With my nightcap on my head;
I don't know if I'm retiring
Or getting out of bed!

So if it's my turn to write to you,
There's no point in getting sore.

I may think that I have written
And don't want to be a bore.

Now I stand before the post box,
With my face so very red.
Instead of mailing you letter –
I have opened it instead!

My bi-focals I can manage,
My dentures fit just fine.
I can turn up my hearing,
But, God! I miss my mind.

After I sent this to my father, so long ago now, I discovered he had written across the top of the page, 'What is so bloody funny about that'?

Not much Dad, wherever you may be, now that I am looking at shuffling off the mortal coil myself. I find in my dotage there are still things I would like to tell him, but he carelessly did not leave his telephone number when he died at the age of 91.

At least my father died. He did not pass away, pass on, enter into the fuller life, depart, pass over to the other side or go to God (he wasn't a believer anyway). I cannot bear the euphemisms for death so well listed in Monty Python's dead parrot sketch. 'Demised, expired, gone to meet his Maker, bereft of life, he's a stiff, resting in peace', or having, 'rung down the curtain on the choir invisible'.

The habit of noting in the local paper the anniversary of a loved one's death still goes on, but not as fulsomely as in days gone by. I saw this one with my own eyes in my alma mater, *The Mercury* last century.

IN MEMORIAM

The angels' trumpets sounded
St Peter called out 'Come!' T
he Pearly Gates swung open A
nd in walked Mum.

Not to forget…

God took our flower,
Our little Nell.
He thought He too
Would like a smell.

And how about this offering in the *The Mercury* to a World War I veteran?

FULTON – In loving memory of a dear son-in-law Athos J Fulton, who died from the effects of the overturning of his motor parlor [sic] coach, Lady Franklin, on the main road, Franklin, on Christmas Day 1928.

Just a memory fond and true,
A loving thought, dear Shat, of you,
An aching heart, a secret tear,
Still keeps your memory ever dear.

Out in a lonely graveyard,
Beneath the cold, cold sod,
There lies a man that was loved by all,
Resting in peace with God.

Gone from us all, that smiling face
Those happy cheerful ways,

The heart that won so many friends,
And died on Christmas Day.
People may think of you being a cripple, dear Shat,
But your artificial limbs made up for all that,
And men with their legs would be few,
To build up a business on that Huon Road such as you.

We thought of how you suffered at the Front for all of us,
And then to think you came back again
To get killed through the brake in that bus.
God murmured, 'Peace be thine'.

So at your grave we should weep not,
Nor think you're lying there;
But turn our faces Heavenward,
Into the sunlit air.

Think how high you are above us,
In the everlasting Spring,
In that Imperial City' And presence of the King'.

....

In the 1970s there was an article published in the in the *Nation Review* claiming that pensioners were so hard up that some had taken to eating canned dog food to survive. This was one response.

DEADLY DOG FOOD

Sir: I am appalled at the sentiments express by John Hepworth on the back page of the Review of 8 January.

The eating of canned dog food is an extremely dangerous practice. To deter your readers from its use, please allow me to state the case of a local man who died after eating pet food for three weeks.

The police recorded his death as an accident, but local residents firmly believe that it was the dogfood that did it.

The poor devil died early one evening after he had been walking home down the middle of the road and when he sat down to lick his dick, a car ran over him.

I recall reading that letter published on 13 February 1972, contributed by Sheila Morgan, of Wingham, New South Wales:

OK I have to admit to believing it until I got to the punchline!

....

Although that was an obvious spoof, over the millennia people have died in wondrously strange ways. I felt it necessary to research some of them. We begin in ancient Greece.

*Draco was the first recorded legislator in Athens. He replaced the prevailing system of oral law and 'blood feud' with written laws that were administered by a court. [Blood feud is a cycle of retaliatory violence, where the relatives of someone who has been killed or wrongfully dishonoured, seek vengeance by killing or injuring the culprits, or their relatives.]

Although Draco was the first democratic legislator for the city state, its citizens were unaware that he would establish tough laws, indeed Draco's laws were so harsh that his work coined the adjective *draconian* which today refers to similarly unforgiving laws in English and other European languages. So it seems odd that in 620 BC he died in a drama theatre on the island of Aegina in connection with a play that was so popular, that in a show of traditional approval (the showering of hats, shirts and cloaks on the head of the actor or playwright concerned) that it smothered him to death!

*And still on drama, Aeschylus the popular playwright of Greek tragedies, was bizarrely killed in 430 BC (according to Valerius Maximus – writer and collector of historical anecdotes) by a tortoise dropped on him by an eagle who had mistaken his bald head for a rock suitable for shattering the shell of the reptile it had captured and taken aloft! For good measure, Pliny later wrote that Aeschylus had been staying outdoors to avert a prophecy that he would be killed by a falling object indoors!

*Pedants should be made aware of the sad fate of the Greek intellectual, Philitas of Cos, who, according to the grammarian Athenaeus, is said to have studied arguments on erroneous word usage so intensively, that he wasted away and starved himself to death in 270 BC.

*In 210 BC the first Emperor of China, Qin Shi Huang, whose artifacts and treasures included the Terracotta Army, died after swallowing several pills of mercury in the belief that it would grant him eternal life. Well, depending on your religious persuasion, he may well have been right!

*The early Christian deacon, Saint Lawrence, fell foul of the Roman Emperor Valerian who in 257 AD commanded Christians to perform sacrifices to the Roman Gods or face banishment, and in the following year toughened that up to lose their property, sent into slavery or be executed. Poor Saint Lawrence was roasted alive on a giant grill for his perceived sins that same year. Prudentius, a Roman Christian poet, later wrote that Saint Lawrence (showing considerable *sang-froid* it must be admitted) joked with his tormentors while being roasted saying, 'Turn me over – I'm done on this side'. Appropriately he is now the patron saint of cooks, comedians and firefighters.

*HA! This is an old favourite. It was George Plantagenet, Duke of Clarence who was allegedly executed by in 1478 by drowning in a barrel of Malmsey wine – at his own request! Better than being roasted on a giant grill I would have thought.

*In 1567 the burgomaster of Branau (then Baravia, now Austria) had the unique distinction of dying after tripping over his own beard. His beard, 1.4 metres long at the time, was usually kept rolled up in a leather pouch.

*Moving into the 20th century, in 1958 actor Gareth Jones collapsed and died between scenes of a live television play, *Underground*, at the studios of the Associated British Corporation in Manchester. Director Ted Kotcheff continued with the play to its end, improvising around Jones' absence. Jones' character, as it happened, was scheduled to have a heart attack – which is what he actually suffered during the performance. Surely that is taking 'method acting' to extremes?

*Garry Hoy, a 38-year-old lawyer in Toronto, Canada, fell to his death on 9 July 1993 after he threw himself against a window on the 24th floor of the Toronto Dominion Centre in an attempt to prove to visitors that the glass was 'unbreakable' – a demonstration he had done many times before. The glass did not break but popped out of the window frame, and Hoy fell to his death.

*In the 21st century there was no shortage of bizarre deaths to report. In 2001, Bernt Brandes, a Berlin engineer, was willingly slaughtered so he could be butchered and eaten by aspiring cannibal, Armin Meiwes. Brandon had replied to an internet advertisement which Meiwes had placed for this purpose!

*The invention of the internet has a lot to answer for. Better fasten your seatbelts for this one. In 2008 a 43-year-old mother of four in Ireland died from having sex with a German Shepherd dog owned by a man she met in an online fetish chatroom. [Presumably shown live on screen to a wider audience.] The semen of the dog triggered a fatal allergic reaction. The owner of the dog was later charged under Ireland's national anti-bestiality laws, the first such case in Irish legal history ever since those laws were passed in 1861.

*In 2013 Joao Maria de Souza, 45, was crushed by a cow falling through the roof of his home in Caratinga, Brazil (the cow having climbed onto the roof from an adjacent steep hillside). His wife, lying in bed beside him, and the cow were both unharmed. Quite understandably the death was labelled as 'bizarre'.

*And finally, in 2014, Peng Fan, a chef in Foshan, China, was bitten by a cobra's severed head, which he had cut off 20 minutes earlier. Fan had set the head aside while using the body to prepare a soup. According to the investigating police, the case was 'highly unusual'. They concluded the chef might have had a severe reaction to the bite!'

I think that is enough, considering these examples are distilled from many, many more.

....

AFTER DEATH US DO PART

Eventually you live long enough to realise that most obituaries, particularly of well-known people, are riddled with cant and hypocrisy. You really need a glossary of terms to bring reality back into the insipid panegyrics so often inflicted on the unsuspecting public. Fellow professionals, for instance, reading about the death of an eminent medico described as 'a grand practitioner of the old school', would know full well that he should have retired years before he did, and was known without affection in the trade as 'that bloody old butcher'.

Let's consider a few more of these euphemisms. For 'gregarious and sports loving' read, 'legendary drunk'. 'Loving husband and father to'… 'a compulsive womaniser'. 'Selfless and lifelong contribution to business' should have been 'a dreadful old crook who couldn't lie straight in bed – or his coffin'.

And that 'self-made man who never lost the common touch' should have been described as 'a ruthless and vulgar opportunist who ate off his knife'.

But the pendulum has been swinging towards refreshing candour in obituaries – in England at any rate. A friend sent me the obituary of one Simon Raven – headlined 'Promiscuous chronicler of upper-class life' – from *The Guardian*, 16 May 2001, and commented: 'You don't see obits like this in Australian papers.' Indeed you don't.

Allow me to share some of Michael Barber's assessment of Mr Raven.

> The death of Simon Raven, at the age of 73 after suffering a stroke, is proof that the devil looks after his own. He ought, by rights, to have died of shame at 30, or of drink at 50.
>
> Instead, he survived to produce 25 novels, *including Alms For Oblivion* (1959-76), a 10-volume saga of English upper-class life, numerous screenplays, eight volumes of essays and memoirs, including *Shadows On The Grass* (1981) – 'the filthiest book on cricket ever written,' according to E W Swanton - and *The First Born Of Egypt* sequence (1984-92), which contains requests such as 'Darling mummy, please may I be circumcised?' and 'Please, sir, may I bugger you, sir?'
>
> How to explain this total one-off character, who combined elements of Flashman, Waugh's Captain Grimes and the Earl of Rochester (though, unlike Rochester, he died an unrepentant pagan)?

The key lies in Simon's love of the classics, which he would read in the original every day. The long hours he spent as a boy 'translating this way and that, from Greek and Latin into English and vice-versa', taught him to write with clarity, precision and wit. Above all, he learned that 'we aren't here for long, and when we do go, that's that. Finish. So, for God's sake, enjoy yourself now - and sod anyone who tries to stop you.'

The story of Simon's early life reads like a Victorian cautionary tale gone wrong. He is the golden youth whose high promise is betrayed by his base appetites, so that one door after another is closed to him. The eldest of three children, he was brought up in 'respectable, prying, puritanical, penny-pinching, joyless' middle-class homes in Virginia Water, Surrey. His father, whom he loathed, had inherited the family hosiery business and did not need to work; his mother, who Simon approved of, was a baker's daughter and a nationally successful athlete.

He later claimed to have been 'deftly and very agreeably' seduced by the games master at Cordwalles preparatory school, near Camberley, but acquired his Luciferian reputation as a scholarship boy at Charterhouse school, before he was expelled in 1945 for serial homosexuality. According to his contemporary, Gerald Priestland, he 'trailed an odour of brimstone'...

After national service in the Parachute Regiment, during which he was sent as an officer cadet to Bangalore and commissioned, Simon arrived, in 1948, to read English at King's College, Cambridge, where he immediately felt at home. "Nobody minded what you did in bed, or what you said about God, a very civilised attitude then," he said...

Debts and dissipation overshadowed Simon's last two years at Cambridge. In 1951, he married Susan Kilner, a fellow undergraduate who was was expecting his child; afterwards, he studiously avoided her, and they were divorced in 1957. After failing to submit a single word of his fellowship thesis, he withdrew from King's and, desperate to flee 'the pram in the hall', successfully applied for a regular army commission.

After three jolly years with the King's Own Shropshire Light Infantry in Germany and Kenya, where he set up a brothel for his men, he was sent home to be training officer at Shrewsbury.

He wrote anything and everything: novels, essays, memoirs and reviews; film scripts, radio plays, television plays and television series, including the 26-episode *The Pallisers* (1974). And if *Alms For Oblivion*, his bleak history of the class of '45, remains his finest achievement, some of his pithiest work was done during the 1960s for *The Spectator*, in whose pages he mocked traditional moralists and trendy egalitarians alike.

Simon had no taste for possessions. In Deal, he had a succession of digs, his only requirement being a landlady who would cook him breakfast and, if required, high tea. His considerable earnings went on food, drink, travel, gambling and sex. He said that one of the unsung advantages of belonging to the Reform Club was the presence opposite of a massage parlour where you got 'a good housemaid's wank'.

He was a generous host, for whom the pièce de resistance was the arrival of the bill, the bigger the better. No matter how much he had eaten and drunk the night before - and his capacity for alcohol was prodigious - he would be at his desk at 9.30 am the following morning.

Tall, slim and beautiful as a youth, Simon soon lost his looks and his figure. He did not repine, rating a good dinner higher than good intercourse. Sexually indiscriminate, he preferred the company of men and believed that a writer, like a soldier, was better accommodated than married with a wife. It was entirely appropriate that he should end his days in the masculine fastness of Sutton's hospital, an Elizabethan alms-house in Charterhouse Square, London.

Simon devised this epitaph for himself: "He shared his bottle - and, when still young and appetising, his bed."

....

O death, where is thy sting. O grave, where is thy victory?

1 Corinthians 15:55

5

THE CHALLENGES OF GETTING IT RIGHT

The communication explosion of recent years with smart phones, Go Pro cameras and the need to be on the spot and on the job 24/7 have eroded the quality of life of the foreign correspondent, as well as home based journalists. The regional ABC offices in South-east Asia, Europe and North America were once the lifeline to the foreign correspondents and stringers, looking after their welfare with help with transport, freelance cameramen (no women in the 20th century), travel admin and on the job expenses.

Africa and Middle East correspondent Sally Sara recently contributed to an ABC-TV's *Foreign Correspondent* documentary titled *Digital Disruption*.

Indeed, particularly since the demise of the regional office, and the need for the correspondent needs to do his or her own filming with a digital camera, or on the ubiquitous mobile phone. When a big story is breaking, the foreign correspondent is expected to take video, audio, sometimes streamed straight to air via satellite, be interviewed on camera for television or on mobile phone for live radio. Correspondents like Sally are expected to stay on their feet performing all these tasks for hours at a time. There is no time to actually research how the story is actually developing because of the continuing need to 'front'.

To get over this, the correspondents often have to be briefed from the news hub in Australia on what has been happening since they began their coverage, because they have had no opportunity to find out for themselves while they have been reporting non-stop.

Sally described in *Foreign Correspondent* once covering action in Kabul, Afghanistan, with intense street fighting and absolutely no back-up. She described filming local street fighting with one hand from a Go

Pro camera, and with the other was giving interviews to ABC radio outlets in Australia on her mobile phone.

This went on for most of the day, and she eventually staggered back to her accommodation to try to get some rest. She checked her computer first of course, to find that her boss had emailed her to say that she was doing a great job, but she had been neglecting her social media outlets,

Sally says she replied, 'How the hell can I do that? Tweet with my toes?'

....

I began my career as a foreign correspondent in the ABC's regional office in Singapore in 1965. It was an exciting time to be posted there. There was *Konfrontasi* [Confrontation] between Indonesia and what President Sukarno considered the British colonial construct of Malaysia (then including Singapore). The British sent troops to defend Malaysia and the former British Borneo provinces of Sarawak and Sabah.

As a rookie war correspondent, I was sent to Borneo to experience that style of jungle warfare, which was an amazing experience. I flew to the capital of Sarawak, Kuching, by De Havilland Comet, the first commercial jet airliners to go into service in 1952. They were withdrawn after several aircraft inexplicably fell out of the air killing all on board. The problems of metal fatigue in jet aircraft were not immediately apparent.

The original Comet aircraft had square windows, and the fatigue started in one corner and opened up the whole aircraft like peeling a banana. The problem was eventually solved, and Comets were flown widely by many airlines in the early 1960s. I flew on a Malaysian Singapore Airlines Comet Mark IV to Borneo (with oval windows). The landing was exciting because the main runway at Kuching was a tad on the short side and didn't leave much margin for error. The pilots used to bang the Comets down onto the runway as quickly as they could and immediately hit reverse thrust.

We shuddered to a halt only metres from the end of the strip. On descent I caught a glimpse of Borneo's extraordinary topography, great mountainranges covered with triple canopy rain forest, except for the huge rivers that looped across the lowlands like great serpents before discharging their brown waters into the otherwise blue South China Sea.

Kuching was a sleepy ex-colonial town that had surged into the news with a plan to 're-settle' the Chinese in the area into what were virtual concentration camps, because of their alleged Communist sympathies.

Singapore, then still federated with Malaysia, took a dim view of this.

The rivers provided the only access to the interior, as they always had even when we were flying by helicopter. The jungle is so dense and forbidding that the choppers flew along the rivers, which at least gave the crews a chance of getting out alive if they had to put down.

As we put on our life-jackets, one of the crew told us that if we went into the river on no account were we to inflate them while we were still in the aircraft, or we'd never get out.

We were bound for Long Jawi, the most isolated military outpost in Sarawak near the Indonesian border. Despite its land locked location, its support base at Nanga Gaat, on the confluence of two rivers, was officially a 'ship' in the naval tradition. As we clattered up the lower reaches of the mighty Rejang River we could see the longhouses of the indigenous people of the region. The Ibans and Dayaks were tough, resourceful people who lived near the rivers where they subsisted on fish and limited rice grown on rough paddy on land reclaimed by burning the jungle.

We were to overnight at Nanga Gaat before flying across the mountains to Long Jawi which was was garrisoned by a Malay regiment. Later that afternoon I found myself water-skiing behind a Royal Navy assault boat driven by a grinning Iban whose brown face and red betel-nut-stained teeth were crowned with a sailor's cap marked *HMS Albion*. The navy pilots were all bearded and wore sarongs.

Their predecessors (who had lived there for two years) went local so enthusiastically they had themselves tattooed in the Iban style. I think they put on their navy combination overalls to fly their helicopters.

It was nightmare flying country. We couldn't take off next morning until the mists lifted to allow us through a saddle in the mountains at

4500 feet [1372 metres]. Our pilot gestured to one of the few emergency landing pads. The top of a mountain had been levelled off into a small cleared area. To achieve this, Ibans had to be lowered down into the jungle that covered even the tops of the mountains to fell trees and slash the undergrowth with parangs and axes so that a small bulldozer could be winched down to flatten off the top of the hill.

The terrain was so rugged it seemed improbable anyone would want to fight a war anywhere near it, but Long Jawi was fortified with trenches and machine-gun posts. It was agreed we would stay the night to film a supply drop from an Argosy cargo plane the next day. The helicopter landing area was so small that a crewman had to guide the pilot down by saying 'Six inches to the left Sir' as he watched our wheels put down gingerly on the tiny pad.

There wasn't much room between the mountains for the Argosy pilot to do his stuff, and the efficiency of the operation wasn't helped by the parachute on the first pallet of supplies failing to open. The pallet came down like a bomb, bursting on impact and scattering the Malay soldiers' personally ordered supplies into the jungle. The next box fell into the river and another was strung up in a tree. In the story I wrote later I commented:

> I know airdrop packers are probably overworked but it does seem to be tempting fate a little to pack bags of cement ON TOP of rice, beer, fruit, brandy, chillies, cigarettes and soap. The resultant mess of those squidged ingredients made a sad sight indeed... On one famous day,' the commanding officer at Long Jawi told me, 'they packed bags of cement on top of a load of eggs'!

We were choppered back to the world's most inland naval station at Nanga Gaat in time for a demonstration of fire-power specially turned on for our camera by the Malay regiment garrisoned there, helped by their naval allies.

Four 45-gallon drums were moored in the middle of the river to represent Indonesian commando boats. The Malay soldiers had first go, and with admirable soldierly restraint, drilled the drums with automatic rifle fire. Then it was the Royal Navy's turn.

With wild yells, saronged and bearded lunatics let fly with their automatic weapons which sounded like the battles of Ypres and the Somme welded into one. One happy warrior blasted off 4000 rounds of machine gun fire (including tracer) in 10 minutes! They kept firing after the drums were well and truly blasted to bits and sunk. Said one beaming piratical-looking pilot, 'I say, that was a bloody good lark, wasn't it? I've been saving up my ammo for MONTHS waiting for a chance like this...'

That evening we were invited to the pictures, projected on to sheets strung between some trees. They showed movies every night! 'Stops us boozing, old boy', said one of the pilots – even though they had seen all the films so often they knew much of the dialogue by heart. We finished up at the Anchor Inn, which boasted a rather splendid swinging door – about which there was a story. Apparently every time a local Iban came in, someone would shout at him, 'Shut the fucking door'. When it became necessary for another hut to be built nearby, they asked for a similar door. The Iban carpenter said through an interpreter, 'Yes Sir, but what kind of door? An ordinary door, or a fucking door?'

A British artillery officer I interviewed later in the northern province of Sabah described the confrontation between Malaysia and Indonesia as 'The last of the fun wars, old boy'. It had all the drama of jungle camps, long and difficult supply lines but hardly a shot fired in anger. The Indonesian soldiers across the border in Indonesian Kalimantan didn't really have their hearts in it, knowing that it was just anti-colonialist posturing by their charismatic president with absolutely no chance of success.

The officer I spoke to in Sabah described it as 'a jolly good show'. But he wasn't sure what war he would fight next. 'We're not in Vietnam, worse luck. Probably be some shower of a country in Africa. That's why I'm enjoying this while it lasts.'

There was a strong air of unreality over the whole affair. The reluctance of the Indonesian Armed Forces, the TNI (*Tentara Nasional Indonesia*) to engage the Malaysian, British and Australian troops stationed in Borneo was confirmed in later years when it was revealed that the TNI literally refused to obey orders from Jakarta during 1963-65 *Konfrontasi*.

Contributing to the Australia and Security Cooperation in the Asia Pacific newsletter of November 2001, Group Captain Ian MacFarling wrote:

> ...the operational commander, General Suharto, in an act of high treason sent emissaries to Kuala Lumpur to explain that the TNI was more interested in defeating the Communists at home than fighting the British Commonwealth on the Indonesian/Malaysian border.

I flew on to Sabah's capital, Jesselton, and finished up at Tawau, about as far as you could get from anywhere in Malaysia but close to where there had been some desultory combat on the Kalimantan border. On the morning of 9 August 1965 I woke in my hotel room and tuned in to Radio Australia for the news, only to discover that Singapore was no longer part of the Federation of Malaysia! This was completely unexpected, and a big story. But I was In Tawau, of all places. Fortunately, experienced hands like my colleague Tony Ferguson were well able to cope without the likes of me, but I was chagrined to be sidelined and away from Singapore at such a time. I hit the phone to organise my flights back.

At breakfast, rather preoccupied with what I had just heard, I saw a British colonel, attached to a Malay regiment, in the dining room. Suspecting – rightly – that he may not have heard the news I thought I should tell him:

> TB: Excuse me, we haven't met, but I thought you might be interested to hear the news that Singapore has broken away from the Federation.
>
> COLONEL: Quite impossible!
>
> TB (nettled): Well, I'm only telling you what I heard on Radio Australia a few minutes ago, and I can assure you that is the case.
>
> COLONEL: I can quite definitely tell you, young man, that such a happening would be quite out of the question.

With that he walked out of the room. Despite the colonel's ostrich-like certainty it was true all right. I made it back to Singapore within 24 hours, which wasn't bad going in the circumstances, but I had missed the main action – the highlight being the 'iron man' of Singapore, Prime Minister Lee, breaking down and crying during his first press conference after the split.

My colleague Tony Ferguson had actually asked the question that had caused this extraordinary reaction. I asked Tony what he had asked Lee. He said it wasn't a particularly penetrating question – he had simply asked the prime minister to outline the recent events that led to the separation. As he did so, Lee broke down – for reasons one can only guess at, but probably the realisation that his dream of one day becoming prime minister of the Federation of Malaysia was over. That dream was one of the main reasons why the Malay administration of Tunku Abdul Rahman in Kuala Lumpur decided to kick Singapore out!

Lee was mortified at his emotional outburst and ordered that the Television Singapura 'pool' film of the press conference be suppressed. But his advisers convinced him that, in Singapore's interest, he should release it. It led news bulletins all over the world.

In Kuala Lumpur there wasn't a peep out of the Malaysian Prime Minister Tunku Abdul Rahman. It was two weeks before his advisers said it was probably time he said something because Lee Kwan Yew was getting all the coverage. This time I was there, and listened in amazement at the press conference while the Tunku described how he had been hospitalised in England having some eye surgery with the added complication of that painful affliction, shingles. Lying in his hospital bed he had mulled over the difficulties in having Singapore, with its 80 per cent Chinese population, inside the Federation, coupled with Lee's political ambitions. (Lee had already enraged Kuala Lumpur by running his People's Action Party candidates in the Malaysian elections in Johore.) The Tunku decided it was all too hard.

Tears seemed far away. The Tunku likened the situation to a couple having problems with their marriage. Giggling happily he explained that when a Malay decided that his wife was incompatible he repeated 'I divorce you' three times. And so he simply said the deal was off. Once was enough.

He didn't even bother to inform the British Government, which had acted as midwife to the Federation. It was touch and go whether Sabah and Sarawak would stay in. Sarawak, with its close Singapore business connections, would not have joined in the first place without Singapore.

It seemed that the break-up of the Federation of Malaysia saga had barely settled before we were all flat out with another huge and breaking story, the attempted Communist coup in Indonesia of 30 September with its attendant massacres of perhaps half a million Indonesian Chinese, suspected Communists and sympathisers, and political and social chaos in Jakarta.

The first we knew of it in Singapore was a news flash on the AAP-Reuter news service. I remember crowding around the teleprinter with my colleagues as the first news started to come through on 1 October 1965. The early stories correctly identified the coup plotters as the 'Thirtieth Of September Movement'. Who the hell were they? Then the coup leader was identified as 'Colonel Qtung'. Alan Morris, an expert speaker of *Bahasa Indonesia* happened to be in the Singapore office preparing to go to Jakarta for Radio Australia. He rightly said that no Indonesian name could possibly begin with 'Q'. It was a teleprinter typo. Colonel Untung was the man of the moment, but not for long. General Suharto was organising a countercoup and the position of President Sukarno was ambivalent, to say the least.

My fellow Tasmanian colleague, Philip Koch, was still operating from the ABC office in Jakarta but his problem was getting his material out. The only way was to 'pigeon' his film, audio tape and uncensored copy to Singapore by going to Jakarta Airport and asking a passenger would he or she mind carrying 'a package for the ABC'. People were astonishingly obliging in this regard. The problem in Singapore was we didn't know which flight Philip's material might be on. We had a roster, going to the airport and importuning arriving passengers from Jakarta once they had passed through customs. 'Excuse me, have you got a package for the ABC?' Often the 'pigeon' was looking out for a contact, which made it easier. Others were less obvious. It was time consuming, tedious, but essential. Imagine that in these days of paranoid security about bombs being carried on to aircraft!

In 1966 the first anniversary of the failed Communist coup was coming up and I went to Jakarta to help cover it then mind the ABC office while Philip had a much needed break.

At that time Indonesia was in chaos, with galloping inflation and an unresolved political situation. What became known as The September 30 Movement acted when it did because of rumours of President Sukarno's failing health. The wily old man was deeply compromised by his support of the Indonesian Communist Party (now defunct) but Indonesia's first president, the man who had welded together the Indonesian nation after Dutch colonial rule – even to the extent of creating a unifying common language *Bahasa Indonesia* – was still widely loved and respected by most Indonesians and his portrait had pride of place on the wall of the humblest *atap* [plaited palm fronds] cottage. Although the President's powers and influence had been much curtailed by the triumvirate of General Suharto, Foreign Minister Adam Malik, and Finance Minister Sultan Hamenko Buwono, they weren't quite confident enough to remove him from the presidency at that stage. Student demonstrations supporting 'The New Order' were growing in strength and militancy, maintaining a rowdy presence at the gates of the *Merdeka* [Freedom] Presidential Palace and President Sukarno was stirring the pot whenever he could, making inflammatory speeches and refusing to go quietly.

The currency had become almost worthless (it was such splendid looking money I papered part of a wall in my Singapore apartment with it) and it was revalued 1000 to 1. There were then old rupiahs and new rupiahs in circulation at the same time with about 115 new Rupiahs to the US dollar, or 115,000 in the old currency. People had to carry around suitcases full of the stuff. Alan Morris, Radio Australia's resident man in Jakarta, stopped to buy some cigarettes from a hawker on his way to work one morning. Alan bargained the price back down to 10 new 'roops' (as they were known), but he only had old roops. Laboriously he began counting out the 10,000 in tattered notes, which took about five minutes, and at the end of this performance the hawker said he owed another 500. 'How come?' asked Alan in fluent *Bahasa*. The seller explained that he had taken so long to count the money that inflation had sent the price up in the interim! Alan was tickled by this cheek and paid over the extra.

Western visitors to Jakarta all stayed at the Hotel Indonesia, one of the few multistorey buildings in the Indonesian capital that was airconditioned and fully functioning. The hotel management didn't muck about with rupiahs – all transactions were in US dollars. The correspondents used to drink in the Ramayana Bar, looking down on the traffic that crawled around the circular pond and fountain in front of the building.

One evening Jack Gillon, a Reuters correspondent, noticed a Pertamina oil tanker grinding its way past the hotel. Oil was one commodity that Indonesia had plenty of, and Sukarno had kept the price of petrol and fuel artificially low. At 15 old roops a gallon [4.5 litres] most petrol outlets wouldn't even bother to collect the insignificant amounts owing. Jack calculated that the two US dollars he'd just paid for his martini in the Ramayana Bar would buy the whole tanker load. Things were in such disarray then and the black market such a fact of life that the Australian Embassy had its own 'official' money changer, and obligingly allowed the ABC to avail itself of this service.

As tensions built towards the failed coup anniversary, Sukarno continued to call press conferences and give speeches at the presidential palace. I went to one of these and was able to see the President, who had a deserved reputation as a great orator, in full flight. Impeccably dressed in military uniform and wearing his trade mark black *pitji* cap, he spoke from a free-standing microphone. He did not need notes. To one side was a small table on which was a glass of fruit juice and a plate of biscuits. This table, apparently, was always there. Sukarno took off his white gloves, laid them and his swagger stick on this little table and moved to the microphone, holding his audience in the palm of his hand even before he started to speak. He began in a low whisper and then, theatrically, built his performance, sometimes quoting in English, Dutch, French or German.

I found it somewhat unnerving that when he broke into English to deliver an epigram from Thomas Carlyle he turned and stared straight at me. His oration was a masterly performance. Standing to one side were the three men, Suharto, Malik and Hamenko Buwono who were currently destabilising him.

I don't know what he said in *Bahasa*, but he pointed to them and said something that made all three smile with some irony. Sukarno was always interested in the foreign press and had noticed my new face among the gaggle of regulars. He asked to meet me and I was introduced to him by Hidayat, the ABC's local interpreter.

He wanted to know the obvious things, what organisation I represented and what I was doing in Indonesia. We made some small talk and he moved on.

As the 30 September anniversary drew closer, the student protests outside the *Merdeka* Palace intensified. The crack Siliwangi Division from outside Jakarta had been brought in for the occasion and they were itching to get their batons on to the shoulders and heads of the students who had been massing outside *Merdeka* Palace for several weeks. I happened to be standing with a group of foreign correspondents, including Phil Koch, in open parkland between the troops and the students.

Suddenly the Palace Guard charged and I turned sideways to switch on my heavy Nagra tape recorder, thinking that they would let us stay where we were. I was wrong. A rifle butt crashed into the small of my back and I looked up to see a very angry soldier, with his bayonet fixed, who seemed to be suggesting I moved on – fast. These soldiers were prepared to use their weapons and there was no safety in being foreign. I shot a sideways glance at Phil Koch being chased by another guardsman with a bayonet inches from his bum. I presumed I had one as close to mine.

It was stinking hot and the tape recorder seemed to weigh a ton as we dashed for the edge of the park fighting for breath, our chests bursting. I hadn't run so fast since school athletics.

This incident signalled a change of tactic by Suharto's army against the demonstrators. Several students were killed in the charge, including two girls. (No guardsmen were reprimanded, nor was there any subsequent apology to parents for the murder of their children.) We were lucky to get out of it unharmed. I hitched a ride on the back of a student's Vespa to get away from the area and back to the office. The troops' action was a message to the students from Suharto that they had better find some other way of protesting.

The process of isolating the President went on for another six months. In March 1967 there was a meeting of the People's Consultative Congress, which only took place every five years. Debate about Sukarno – whether he was a traitor and should be put on trial, or whether he should remain as Indonesia's honoured president and father of the revolution – went on for five days. At the end the conference chairman, General Nasution, announced that Sukarno would no longer be known as 'President' but would be called Dr 'Engineer' Sukarno.

There was still a nervousness about sacking the old man and General Suharto had to clarify the findings of the congress, telling the press that Sukarno would be treated 'as a president who is no longer in power'. Dr Engineer Sukarno, by then in very poor health, retired to his favourite palace at Bogor in the hills outside Jakarta. He remained under virtual house arrest as the Suharto's 'New Order' regime consolidated its power. He died in Jakarta on 21 June 1970.

After the brouhaha of the first anniversary of the attempted coup died down, I was keen to venture into the interior of Java to find out what I could about the post-coup killings, the extent of which will never be accurately known, but which vary from 200,000 to several million. How much of this slaughter was anti-Communist, attempted genocide against Indonesia's ethnic Chinese or simply the settling of old scores is impossible to know. That there was a frenzy of killing there is no doubt. Rivers were clogged and choked with bodies.

Taking Alan Morris to translate and a driver, we drove in a venerable, big black Buick from Jakarta through central Java to Bali. (Our fuel costs were modest – a total of five US dollars, due to the farcical, controlled fuel prices. Most garages did not even bother to take the worthless 'roops'). The people in the villages and towns we drove through seemed subdued. I found later that we had been lucky not to encounter militant black-shirted youth groups still loyal to President Sukarno. They would have seen us as imperialist lackeys. Unsurprisingly there was not a tourist to be seen so the hotels *en-route* were very pleased to see us.

I was particularly keen to get to Bali, not only for its legendary charms but because my colleague Neil Davis had told me that the killings there had been particularly bad. The Communists had been found guilty of disturbing the carefully balanced Hindu-Buddhist rhythm of village life and communal harmony. This was regarded as a great crime. Councils of village elders tried the Communists and ordered that they be executed – usually by decapitation. There had been group slaughter as well, probably used as an excuse to settle old scores. It seemed difficult to believe that this had happened in serene Bali, of all places.

I found an American missionary who was prepared to talk to me on tape about what had happened. He estimated that on the small island of Bali alone, 70 000 people had been executed or murdered. We looked around for a quiet place to record and sat down on a mound of earth, in the shade of a tree. As we talked, a group of locals gathered around to watch what was going on. After we finished and I was packing up my recorder, one of the group came over spoke something in Balinese to the missionary. He looked startled.

'That man told me that the mound of earth we were sitting on is the mass grave of 17 murdered communists.'

....

At this time the Vietnam war was escalating, with President Johnson building up American forces to 500,000 to combat the Viet Cong in South Vietnam. These were being supported by North Vietnamese tough and battle-hardened troops who had not long before forced the occupying French colonial regime out of their country.

They now planned to do the same with the Americans and other nations like South Korea and Australia who had also contributed their troops to fight the communists.

My first experience of Vietnam had been in November 1965. I was sent there not specifically to report on the war, although that came later, but to record Christmas messages on tape from Australian Diggers to be broadcast on the ABC to their families in Australia.

This quaint tradition dated back to World War II and was already an anachronism as the Diggers could tape their own messages. The first Philips cassette tape recorders had just come on to the market and every duty-free store and US military PX was full of them.

(I recorded a 1965 Christmas message to the folks at home from this young Australian artillery corporal in Malaya. Tape recorders were becoming more portable slung over my shoulder, although the club-like microphones were still quite alarming. The machine was a Swiss Stellavox, with small 6.5 centimetre diameter spools of long-play tape that only ran for about eight minutes with luck. Not sure why I was wearing a tie!)

Although Australian warrant officer advisers had been in Vietnam for several years working with Vietnamese troops in most of the combat areas of South Vietnam, the first detachment of regular troops (1 RAR) had only arrived in May 1965. They had not then been assigned to their operational area, Phuoc Tuy Province, but were working with two battalions of the United States 173rd Airborne Battalion, defending the big the Bien Hoa air base, about 45 kilometres north-east of Saigon.

Saigon's Tan Son Nhut airport in late 1965 was one of the busiest in the world, its limited runways coping with jet fighters, lumbering C130 transports, commercial airliners, Cessna artillery spotting planes and the ubiquitous Huey helicopters their rotors producing that distinctive 'thwok thwok thwok' sound which I will forever associate with the Vietnam war. A familiar tall, blond-headed, debonair figure, Neil Davis, bless his heart, was at the airport to meet me and spirited me through the narrow Saigon streets crammed with motor cyclos, battered Peugeot taxis, jeeps and heavy military vehicles – to say nothing of the thousands of cyclists somehow making their way through it all. Despite all that Saigon, still had a certain vestige of French charm with its outdoor cafes and striped umbrellas, although some places featured ugly, sandbagged blast walls as well. The Viet Cong's policy of never allowing US soldiers to feel safe wherever they were was a policy in operation well before the Tet uprising of 1968 and the Floating Restaurant on the Saigon River, where western-ers tended to congregate, was blown up, crowded with lunchtime diners, shortly before I arrived. (Street urchins used to give GIs palpitations by sneaking up to cafes and bars and rolling in Coke cans filled with gravel – then run off giggling as terrified soldiers threw themselves on the floor.)

Neil introduced me to Dema, a nervous Indian moneychanger who occupied what looked like a large cupboard in the Visnews office in central Saigon. (It was typical of Davis to have his own black market money man living in.) I changed some US dollars for a wadge of Vietnamese pias-tres (known colloquially as 'disasters') and was then spirited through the accreditation process by Neil (who knew everyone) for both the Army of the Republic of South Vietnam (ARVN) and the United States Military Assistance Command Vietnam (MACV). Journalists covering the war had a lot of clout. I think my press pass gave me the equivalent rank of a lieutenant and I was just a blow-in.

My ABC colleague Don Simmons, who was assigned to Vietnam full time, said his MACV pass gave him the honorary rank of captain! With the US policy of openness in allowing the press to cover the Indo China war in full swing I could even bump serving soldiers off helicopters to get a ride if I was silly enough to do so. (This was the last 'open' war for correspondents ever allowed by the United States.)

Later that day I made contact with Don Simmons, who had invited me to stay in his flat, about 10 minutes drive to the north of central Saigon. He also said I could use the office jeep which was painted white and looked like a United Nations vehicle. Don said it was handy for driving after the 10 pm curfew – the police were likely to stop you and ask questions instead of firing first. I thought it unwise to test this out, but Don said he had.

Neil Davis hadn't paid a great deal of attention to the arrival of the Australians as he was focussing his camera lenses on a bigger canvas. As early as 1964 he had formed the opinion that the Vietnam war would be won or lost on the ground by Vietnamese troops, despite President Johnson sending half a million US soldiers to Indo China by 1966.

He also knew, as a one-man-band, that he couldn't compete with the resources of the major US television networks who concentrated only on covering what the Americans were doing. So he went out with the South Vietnamese army who did not have the luxury of helicopter evacuations in the event of being wounded in action.

This meant going on patrol for up to a week, carrying all his own equipment, eating Vietnamese army rations and drinking paddy water, albeit with a touch of chlorine.

He was the only western cine-cameraman to do this and as a result had that side of the conflict all on his own. He carried a spring-loaded Bell and Howell camera (which needed no batteries) and one of the new cassette tape recorders strapped to his waist for wild sound.

Neil got on famously with the South Vietnamese (ARVN) troops with whom he conversed easily in a patois of South Vietnamese, French and English. They also taught him the basics of surviving in this style of combat.

Unbelievably, he continued to cover front line action in Vietnam and Cambodia for 11 years, despite being wounded several times, once seriously. His unique combat film enabled the British news film agency Visnews not only to compete with the US networks which showed only American-related action, but also to show the world that most of the fighting in Indo China was being done by Asian troops, who sustained horrendous casualties.

(In 1985 Neil Davis was killed by shrapnel in the streets of Bangkok, covering an attempted coup on 9 September. I wrote his biography *One Crowded Hour – Neil Davis Combat Cameraman, 1934-85*, first published in 1987.)

Strangely in those early years there was considerable optimism that the overwhelming force and firepower of the US forces MUST be able to defeat the 'black-pajama clad peasant soldiers' and defeat the Communists in the interests of the free world. But this was before the Viet Cong uprising during the religious festival of TET in 1968, when a holiday from combat was supposed to be observed by all sides changed the course of the Vietnam war for ever. The Vietcong even captured and held, for some hours, the US Embassy in Saigon!

The Americans failed to take into account that the North Vietnamese tough, battle-hardened troops had already seen off their French colonial masters and planned to do the same with the Americans. They were also well supplied by both China and the Soviet Union with arms, munitions and even tanks!

There was also a distressing ambivalence between the Americans' attitudes to the Vietnamese they were supposed to be assisting, as the language barrier remained impenetrable to most GIs. As Neil Davis pertinently said, these GIs, regarded the South Vietnamese Army not as fellow human beings, but as 'funny little animals running around'.

While the Americans routinely burnt down villages thought to have hidden Viet Cong fighters, they also tried to 'win the hearts and minds of the people' by assisting them with agriculture and other aid. It was not a happy mix. This program had the unfortunate acronym of WHAMMO. I heard of one GI in the Delta region of South Vietnam who had a sign on his combat helmet: LET ME WIN YOUR HEART AND MIND OR I'LL BURN YOUR FUCKING HOUSE DOWN.

The infamous My Lai Massacre in March 1968 when between 400 and 500 men, women and children were killed (including infants) and women raped before they were slaughtered, was the worst atrocity of the whole war committed against Vietnamese civilians. This did not come to light until 1969, and those responsible were never brought to justice. The leader of C Company, Lieutenant William Calley, did not serve gaol time, but three- and-a-half years under house arrest!

....

For the foreign correspondents in the 1960s, communications were extremely primitive. Radio coverage had to rely on scratchy sound transmitted through undersea cables. News stories dispatched as cables sent by Morse code, and film taken in the field by a cameraman and sound technician had to be sent back to Singapore for processing then flown either to Europe for the international news agency VISNEWS or to Australia for editing and then all States.

At that stage, only Sydney, Canberra and Melbourne were connected by coaxial cable for simultaneous transmission. Brisbane, Adelaide, Perth and Hobart (known in ABC jargon as the 'BAPH' states) had to go it alone.

As I worked for Current Affairs Radio (as well as ABC News) I had a roving brief to spread myself over South-east Asia including Malaysia, Thailand, Laos, Indonesia, Vietnam and the Philippines. Looking back, I enjoyed the last of the good times where a correspondent could advise Head Office that he would be out of touch for, say, a week and then gather (in my case) tape-recorded interviews and sometimes the sound of battles, or more peaceful forays like the elections in the Philippines to cover the elec-tion that put President Marcos in power in 1966.

For me this was the time the rot started to set in for me with the beginning of the explosion of instant communications.

As I mentioned earlier, our stories were still quaintly sent by cable, by Morse code, like extended telegrams. One morning I went down to the General Post Office to file my cable, full of cable-ese like MANILA EXBOWDEN UPDATE ELECTION STOP. You were charged by the word, so the convention was to run words together whenever possible, mangling the English language with words like 'UNPROCEED' instead of 'do not go' and so on.

(One foreign correspondent for a British newspaper once resigned his job by cable, which of course, he had to pay for himself, by the word. He famously cabled his long-suffering news editor in London, 'UPSTICK JOB ARSEWARDS', thereby saving five words!)

Back in Manila, I handed over my cable in the Post Office and the telegraphist said, 'Why don't you send it by Telex'? 'What's that,' sez I? I don't recall exactly what he said, but he did say it was quicker. I'll say it was. I hung about for a few minutes to buy some stamps, and was just walking out when he said: 'Oh just a minute Mr Bowden, Sydney a query on your story... 'Sydney has a WHAT?' The awful realisation dawned that this indeed was instant communication. 'Tell them I've left'! This was much too close for comfort. I knew that life was going to get more hectic for the foreign correspondent in future, and I was right.

....

In a previous chapter I mentioned that London's Fleet Street news-papers employed distinguished and extremely experienced correspon-dents to literally cover the world if the story was big enough. In Evelyn Waugh's wonderful satire on journalism, *Scoop*, one such exalted being was Sir Jocelyn Hiscock. Waugh wrote that on one occasion Hiscock took the wrong flight and landed unexpectedly in a small African land-locked country he did not intend to visit. His reputation was such, that the mere fact he had arrived in the country caused a revolution and toppled the government.)

One of the great journalist figures of the post-war, and into the 1970s, was the London *Daily Mirror's* Donald Wise. He cut a dashing figure, over six feet tall, with a David Niven style moustache and a super pukka accent. He was an ex-British paratrooper who had been a prisoner of war of the Japanese in Changi and on the Burma Railway, where he had got to know, and fortunately like, Australians.

I first met him in Vietnam in 1966 through a colleague Neil Davis, who was a great friend of his. As with journalists in most situations, and particularly in a war, there was a deal of black humour in the trade to insulate you from the awfulness of what was going on.

And in this case it was pretty awful. The Thieu/Ky Government in Saigon had decided to crack down on war profiteering – a bit of a sick joke in itself really, as the government hierarchy was known to be on the take. There was a strong racist element too, as the decision was made to execute Chinese Vietnamese as alleged war profiteers. Taking little account of what the Western world might think, they began executing

Chinese businessmen by firing squad in the market place at 8 am every day. You can imagine what a public relations triumph this turned out to be.

Still pictures and film of distraught widows and children trying to crawl over coils of barbed wire to get to their husbands and fathers, their riddled bodies slumping against the execution posts were seen worldwide.

Donald Wise had been out of the country while this had been going on and didn't know about it. Neil Davis picked him up from the airport and said nothing. They chatted casually as they drove into the city - past the sandbagged execution points. 'What's that,' said Donald?

'Oh that's where they have been having public executions of Chinese war profiteers', said Neil offhandedly. 'Have you seen it,' asked Donald? 'Filmed it', said Neil. 'They did five in one go last Saturday morning.' There was a long silence. 'Christ' said Donald. 'You have all the luck!'

....

The first Australian combat unit, 1 RAR, arrived in Vietnam in March 1965. They were first sent to the big US Bien Hoa air base, just outside Saigon, where they were put under canvas near the American troops already guarding the complex. When I got to Vietnam for the first time some months later, I thought I had better try to do some stories on the Australian operations. This proved much harder than I thought. First I had to buy some suitable clothing, jungle greens and so on. I went to the famous Khu Dan Sinh black market in Saigon where it was said you could buy anything, from a helicopter still in its original boxes to cut price Scotch. I had no problem picking up some jungle greens that I hoped would enable me to blend in with the soldierly crowd, plus belts, water bottles and jungle boots, hoping their previous owner hadn't died in them. The Australians weren't all that pleased to see me. The army has always had an ambivalent attitude towards the press, to put it mildly, and were appalled by the Americans' friendly treatment of the reptiles of the press. The Australian Army's HQ staff's instinctive response to visiting newsmen was to accord them the status of the Viet Cong. When the Australians first arrived at

Bien Hoa air base, some American correspondents went down to see what their new allies were doing, and were bewildered by the Australians' attitude to them.

So they went next door to their own 173rd Airborne battalion, simply asked what the Australians were doing, and were told.

The Australian Army was forced to rethink their approach to public relations, but they still hated the press.

Not long after 1RAR went to Bien Hoa, Australian correspondents were agitating to be taken out on a patrol. This was resisted until the Australian command was forced to make some token gestures. Creighton Burns, from *The Age*, Melbourne, was in Saigon at that time and was one of the first correspondents to be taken on a perimeter daylight patrol.

Fellow Australians Alan Ramsey and photographer Stuart McGladrie (who were living in the 1 RAR camp) were there for AAP, and had to pay a dollar a day for their food, even though they were allotted a tent within the Australian camp. Knowing this, Creighton Burns thought it safer to bring his own tucker.

The Battalion CO Colonel Lou Bromfield told Creighton that he did not think the patrol would run into anything nasty. In fact there was no chance of action because the Australian Army detested and resisted having to take civilians into fighting territory. When they stopped for lunch, Creighton unwrapped a brown paper parcel he had been carry-ing and produced his meal – a crusty French loaf, some Camembert cheese, sliced *jambon* and a fresh tomato, all beautifully wrapped in a white, damask napkin.

He even had a half bottle of *vin rouge*. He shared some with the Diggers, who admitted it was a lot better than their US Army C rations. It also pointed up the utter futility of the so-called 'patrols' that the press would be permitted to cover.

Some months later Creighton heard that 1 RAR was about to go out with the US Airborne Brigade into an area known as War Zone D, which promised some real action with the Viet Cong.

At that time he was sharing an apartment in Saigon with Donald Wise, the correspondent for the London *Daily Mirror*. Wise was not unused to combat, having been a paratrooper with the British forces in World War Two, and commanded a platoon of Iban trackers during the Malayan Emergency. Burns persuaded him that his readers would relish a story about the Australian Diggers in action.

Things did not start well. The two men stepped out of their helicopter at the Australian headquarters, Wise debonair in a spotted camouflage jacket he had managed to get from the Vietnamese Rangers he had also recently visited. A couple of Australian Diggers were leaning against a palm tree watching this arrival. In Donald's hearing, one said to the other, 'Christ we're saved mate. Fucken' Tarzan's here'.

They were met at the Australian camp by a public relations major who said it was not possible for them to cover the action.

Pressed why, he said there were not enough field rations. Creighton responded, saying that if they didn't take them, they would go with the Americans who were in control of the operation anyway, and they would both write stories saying 1 RAR was nervous about being seen in action. The major looked edgy and invited them to have dinner at the officers mess.

Inside the large mess tent four or five young officers were having dinner.

Creighton doubted if any of them had yet heard a shot fired in anger. The PR major introduced them and asked that they be made welcome. As they sat down, all the officers ostentatiously moved further down the table.

Creighton Burns was deeply embarrassed. Wise smiled, and said in a voice loud enough to be heard, 'What did you say the motto of this battalion was, dear boy – 'Feel free to fuck off'? Creighton made sure the story got about to other correspondents and Donald's description became the catch cry of journalists trying to do business with the Australians.

There had been official acceptance of my Christmas messages assignment, so I was given a stretcher in a tent and grudging cooperation. I wandered about with my tape recorder asking Diggers if they wanted to send messages home to their folks.

Most said no, because they'd sent off their own recorded cassettes. I had prepared a sample pro-forma. 'My name is John Smith, and I'm speaking from Bien Hoa air base in South Vietnam. Hello Mum and Dad, I'd just like to say how much I'll be missing you all this Christmas, and wish you all the best. It's pretty hot here at the moment... I went on leave in Saigon last week and had a massage and a fuck... (That was probably true, but not actually in my sample message.) Well that's about all I can think of to say at this moment, so once again, a merry Christmas to all the family.'

A few of the Diggers actually read out the sample message I'd written. I got myself back to Saigon as soon as I had recorded enough messages to fulfil my ludicrous assignment. I never did it again after writing a fairly savage report to the ABC on the futility of this World War II historical anomaly.

....

I interviewed Donald Wise in later years about what he considered his most dangerous moment as a foreign correspondent.

It was in 1960 in the Belgian Congo, just after he had moved from *the Daily Express* to the London *Daily Mirror*. In the anarchy of the former Belgian Congo in those days, a former Sergeant of the Katanga Police, one Norbert Mouke, promoted himself to a general, commanding the Katanga gendarmerie. Mouke, Donald said, was a very limited man indeed, and called a press conference, which was handled by his Belgian adviser.

He was wearing a British army parachute regiment cap and badge which infuriated Donald because he clearly had never been in any parachute regiment let alone a British one. Eventually General Mouke stood up and addressed the meeting.

Now Mouke was a shortish man with bandy legs, and he was wearing what in the British army call a Denison Smock – a parachute smock in camouflage material, with a tail that hung down, that was pulled through your legs and clipped it to the front. This was to stop the smock or jacket from flying over your head when you jumped from an aircraft. Wise:

Mouke wore very short shorts, and he stood with his legs apart and his arms folded, looking very severe. When the photographers asked him to smile, he said: 'I don't smile, I'm a serious man'.

He was that kind of bloke. Well, there he was standing there with his bandy black legs and this bloody great tail of the Denison Smock hanging down between them. You couldn't see any shorts of anything, and he really looked quite simian.

He went on and on pontificating and we were all getting very restless. I incautiously and very rudely said: 'For God's sake somebody throw the General a banana'. And, of course, just at that moment nobody was talking, and it was a remark that I thought would get us all shot. I mean he got very angry, and the press conference came to an end. It was a preposterous remark, and I do think that was my most dangerous moment.

I think one of the stories that gave Donald most journalistic satisfaction was one he placed in the London *Daily Mirror* from Vietnam in 1970 that no other journalist could write for their paper, and took bets on the side that Donald couldn't get it in his! It also says something about how prudish papers were in those days about something that would be published without difficulty today in the mainstream press. The story tells itself and I quote... but first the headline:

From Donald Wise in Saigon

The American soldier in Vietnam was miles away from the front line when he received a wound which won him a Purple Heart medal.

He was, in fact, relaxing in a massage parlour when the enemy put the bite on him. The enemy was a masseuse. And the wound she gave the GI was a love bite on 'a very tender spot'.

Later it was discovered the masseuse was a Vietcong agent. Her love bite was promptly labelled 'hostile action' and the GI qualified for the Purple Heart – the medal awarded to American servicemen wounded in action.

The story of the bitten soldier was revealed yesterday in the Pacific edition of the GI Newspaper *Overseas Weekly*. The paper said that the GI, a member of the US 25th Division, was in the steam bath when the masseuse bit him. When the bite became infected he reported sick and told his story to the medical officer.

Army authorities asked Vietnamese police to trace the girl, and she turned out to be a Vietcong agent who was under surveillance.

The Overseas Weekly said: 'Everybody has heard of guys getting Purple Hearts under strange or doubtful circumstances, but this one has to take first place. We wonder how they worded the citation?

....

ANYONE HERE BEEN RAPED AND SPEAKS ENGLISH?

One of the greatest problems for journalists writing a memoir is to think of an arresting title. The prize I think has to go to Edward Behr for his: *Anyone here been raped and speaks English* in which he speaks of his experiences in the Belgian Congo in the 1960s, first published in 1978.

(When I first heard of this book, I was told that title was *Has any nun who has been raped here speaks English* but that was not so, although some unfortunate nuns in the departure lounge almost certainly had been.)

The scene was Kinshasha Airport, Congo, stinking hot, with terrified Belgian refugees waiting for flights to Europe. Many had been driven out of remote up-country towns by excesses of Congolese soldiers on the rampage.

> In the middle of this crowd strode an unmistakably British TV reporter, leading his cameraman and sundry technicians like a platoon commander through hostile territory. At intervals he paused and shouted, in a stentorian but genteel BBC voice, 'Anyone here been raped and speaks English'?

> (I would like to include in the genre of memorable memoir titles the Australian author John Birmingham's effort, *Don't tell mum I work on the oil rigs...she thinks I'm a piano player in a whorehouse.*)

Edward Samuel Behr (born in Paris on 7 May 1926 and died, also in Paris, on 27 May 2007) was a foreign and war correspondent. His early career as a reporter was with Reuters in London and Paris. Later he joined Time-Life as Paris correspondent, and in the late 1950s and early 1960s often covered the fighting in the Congo, the civil war in Lebanon as well as the Indo-Chinese border clashes of 1962. He wrote about the unrest in Ulster, the fighting in Angola and the Moroccan attack on Ifni, the Spanish enclave in West Africa.

Returning to India for *Time* magazine, Behr served as bureau chief in New Delhi, travelled in Indo-China, then moved to the mass-circulation American magazine *The Saturday Evening Post* as roving correspondent. In 1965 he went to *Newsweek*, the weekly news magazine owned by the Washington Post Company.

Operating from Hong Kong as Asia bureau chief, Behr wrote on China's Cultural Revolution, secured an interview with Mao Zedong and reported from Vietnam. The year 1968 turned out to be a hectic one for Behr – he was in Saigon during the Tet offensive, in Paris for the student riots and in Prague when it was occupied by the Russians.

Behr turned gradually from a career in war reporting to writing books and making television documentaries, including award-winning programs on India, Ireland and the Kennedy family. A notable production was *The American Way of Death*, Behr's look at America's undertaking industry.

I think it can be said he won his journalistic spurs. But to return briefly to the Congo. Behr:

A United Nations force came in to the Congo. Included an Irish battalion, which arrived in the tropics with First World War woollen uniforms and puttees.

An Irish soldier was killed by some Baluba tribesmen, leading to the story, that went the rounds of the bars wherever correspondents gathered in the Congo, that on being told that her son had been strung up by the Balubas, his aged mother had replied:

'They shouldn't have done that. There was no call to hang him up by the balubas'.

Behr later wrote that a lot of people weary journalists with the cliche about 'what an interesting life you must lead'. In 1969 Pope Paul VI visited Holy Land, and toured Jerusalem. Georges Ménager, a *Paris Match* photographer was assigned to cover the tour. At one point there was such a densely cheering crowd police could not get the Pope through – and had to clear a path.

While they tried to beat back the faithful, Pope Paul VI and Ménager, isolated from the crowd and the rest of the press corps, eyed each other warily. Finally the Pope said in his fluent but heavily accented French, 'What an interesting life you must lead'. Ménager stared back and grunted, 'You haven't done so badly either'.

Reporters and photographers an odd bunch. Behr again:

Sitting in a beleaguered Belfast hotel several winters ago, a world-famous war photographer outlined this dilemma in an apt if somewhat crude, stream-of-consciousness monologue.

'All I want right now,' he said, 'is to be in my semidetached bungalow in Surbiton surrounded by my dear wife and three screaming children. And when I'm there, I know what I'll really want is to wrestle with that marvellous little whore who used to share my nights when I was last in Vientiane'.

Later Behr was in Nigeria, where he watched a British television crew filming shortly after the collapse of the Biafra secessionists.

A wave of robberies was being repressed by the government in the most brutal way possible – by capital punishment – and the crew was filming an execution. The unfortunate victim, convicted of some particularly modest robbery, had been tied to a tree and blindfolded.

A priest had administered the last rites. An army squad, its rifles loaded, took aim. At this point the proceedings were interrupted by the sound engineer. 'Stop everything, please', he said. 'There's something wrong with the set.'

The execution squad commander courteously obeyed; the troops grounded arms until the tinkering with the recorder was completed. 'Now let's have a test,' the sound engineer said, completely oblivious of his surroundings. 'OK, you can go ahead now.'

....

THINGS ON RADIO THAT MIGHT HAVE BEEN BETTER EXPRESSED

Jon Snow: 'In a sense, Deng Xiaoping's death was inevitable, wasn't it?" Expert: 'Er, yes.' (Channel 4 News)

As Phil De Glanville said, "each game is unique, and this one is no different to any other." (John Sleightholme BBC1)

'If England are going to win this match, they're going to have to score a goal.' (Jimmy Hill BBC)

'Beethoven, Kurtag, Charles Ives, Debussy - four very different names.' (Presenter, BBC Proms, Radio 3)

'Julian Dicks is everywhere. It's like they've got eleven Dicks on the field.' (Metro Radio Sports Commentary)

Listener: 'My most embarrassing moment was when my artificial leg fell off at the altar on my wedding day.'

Interviewer Simon Fanshaw: ' How awful! Do you still have an artificial leg?' (Talk Radio)

Interviewer: 'So did you see which train crashed into which train first?' Fifteen-year-old boy: Er, no – they both ran into each other at the same time. (BBC Radio 4)

Presenter (to palaeontologist): "So what would happen if you mated the woolly mammoth with, say, an elephant?"

Expert: 'Well in the same way that a horse and a donkey produce a mule, we'd get a sort of half-mammoth.'

Presenter: 'So it'd be like some sort of hairy gorilla?' Expert: 'Er, well yes, but elephant-shaped, and with tusks.'

Interviewer Kilroy-Silk: 'Did you mean to get pregnant?' Girl: 'No, It was a cock-up.'

Grand National winning jockey Mick Fitzgerald: 'Sex is an anti-climax after that!'

Desmond Lynam: 'Well, you gave the horse a wonderful ride, everyone saw that.' (BBC)

....

FINAL REFLECTIONS ON JOURNALISM BY
ITS PRACTITIONERS

'The purpose of interviewing is to gain trust in order to betray it,' (US journalist Janet Malcolm)

'You are only as good as your last fuckup'. (Art Lord NBC News)

6

LIFE WITH AUNTY

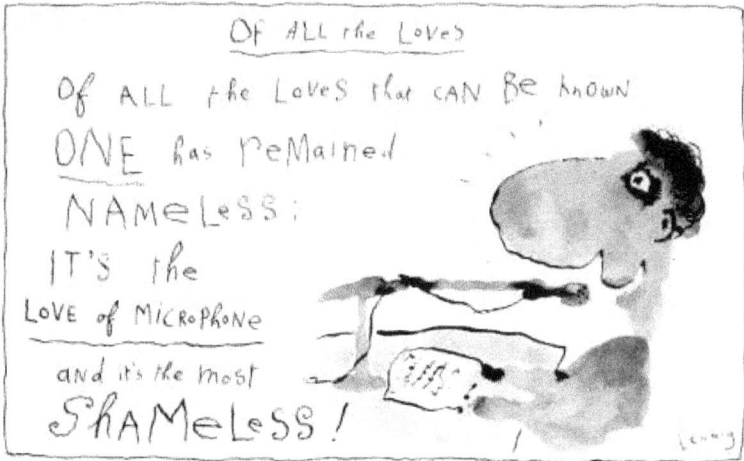

Of ALL the Loves

Of ALL the Loves that CAN Be known
ONE has remained
NAMeless:
IT's the
LOVE of MICRoPhoNe
and it's the most
ShAMeLeSS!

I worked on the staff of 'Aunty' ABC (the Australian Broadcasting Commission, later Corporation) for 29 years and 11 months, not quite making it to 30. In fact I worked for the ABC for longer, beginning in Hobart Tasmania as a freelance broadcaster from 1958 until 1960 when I left for England and freelanced for the BBC General Overseas Service (later World Service) in London in 1961 and 1962 – so I was employed by both Aunties.

The BBC first earned the Aunty tag under the stern reign of its first director general John Reith, who created the public broadcaster during his stewardship from 1927 to 1938, retiring the year after I was born. (He had started with the British Broadcasting Company Ltd earlier, as its general manager from 1922 and managing director until 1927.) The ABC inevitably became known as Aunty too, as it was created very much in the BBC's image, as a public broadcaster untainted by commercialism and designed to bring education and enlightenment to the great unwashed.

It is said that the 'Aunty' image was a Reithian concept to reflect his wishes that the BBC would broadcast nothing that might upset his (fictitious) maiden aunt. This impression was most likely strengthened by the British comedian Kenny Everett in the 1960s who with mock affection spoke of 'Aunty Beeb', likening the broadcaster's censorious attitudes to those of a repressed maiden aunt. Reith was a towering figure physically. He was six foot six in tall [193.12 centimetres] and maintained a stern demeanour.

He created the templates for public service broadcasting in England and Australia, fought off politicians' attempts to influence the BBC while offering programs he believed would inform, educate and entertain – in that order.

In the early years of the 1930s, the sculptor Eric Gill was commissioned to carve an image of a sower for the entrance hall of Broadcasting House. 'Broadcast' is the old word for scattering seed – you cast it far and wide and good things grow.

As a preacher stands in the pulpit and hopes that the congregation will be improved by the word of God, so John Reith the minister's son cast the seeds of virtue into Britain. The Latin inscription in the hallway of Old Broadcasting House, through which workers still hurry to their offices at Radios 3 and 4, translates:

> *This temple of the arts and muses is dedicated to Almighty God by the*
> *first Governors in the year of our Lord 1931, John Reith being direc-*
> *tor-general. And they pray that good seed sown may bring forth good*
> *harvest, and that all things foul or hostile to peace may be banished*
> *thence, and that the people inclining their ear to whatsoever things are*

lovely and honest, whatsoever things are of good report, may tread the path of virtue and wisdom.

And he ruled with an iron hand, taking a keen interest in everything that was broadcast. For example Harold Nicolson confided to his diary his frustrations about Reith. They had been discussing a series of talks on modern literature he was to give. 'The man's head is made entirely of bone ... he tries to induce me to modify my talks in such a way as to induce the illiterate members of the population to read Milton instead of going on bicycle excursions. I tell him that as my talk series centres upon literature of the last 10 years it would be a little difficult to say anything about Milton.'

From the earliest days of the BBC, the balance between the popular and the niche has been fiercely contested. 'To have exploited so great a scientific invention for the purpose and pursuit of 'entertainment' alone would have been a prostitution of its powers and an insult to the character and intelligence of the people,' wrote Reith in his 1924 book *Broadcast Over Britain*.

Some listeners took a different view. In the first issue of the *Radio Times*, 28 September 1923, a reader's letter commented: 'Frankly, it seems to me that the BBC are mainly catering for the "listeners" who... pretend to appreciate only and understand only highbrow music and educational and "sob" stuff. Surely, like a theatre manager, they must put up programs which will appeal to the majority and must remember that it is the latter who provide the main bulk of their income.'

Why does the BBC bother with niche culture, to be enjoyed only by a few, some ask? Others wonder why it promulgates mass culture which, it is argued, the market could provide.

'His name is still a byword for high-minded broadcasting. But Lord Reith was an adulterer and family tyrant who was so profligate he left just £75 in his will. Who says so? His own daughter...'
Frances Hardy, Daily Mail

The fierce alleged moral rectitude of Lord John Reith was badly dented in 2007 when his only daughter, Marista Leishman, then in her 70s, published her account of life with her formidable father, *My Father: Reith of The BBC*. For all his outward pretence of stern morality, he was in fact a hypocrite according to his own daughter. Publicly, she says, he abhorred infidelity, but privately he enjoyed relationships with a series of malleable young women - and once, while in his 20s, even had an intimate liaison with a man.

The untold story during Reith's lifetime was his deep affection for a younger man, Charlie Bowser, whose family lived near the Manse in Glasgow. There is no clear proof that it was a homosexual relationship, though Reith's biographer Ian McIntyre believes it was. When their relationship ended, Reith destroyed many of the relevant sections of his diary and got rid of Charlie's letters. But even the expurgated recollections tell of times when they swam naked together, shared a bed and kissed. And while people today are less likely to take a moral stand on homosexuality – a criminal act at the time – they might be less indulgent about the way Reith used his influence to get the young man jobs. He even proposed him for an OBE!

Reith's stock-in-trade was fomenting shock and outrage. In the prelude to World War II, he brazenly expressed his admiration for Hitler and, later, his detestation of Churchill, whom he numbered in a list of his seven most hated men. Meanwhile, his own personality – tyrannical, self-centred and riddled with paradoxes – bore more than a passing resemblance to that of a dictator.

His daughter Marista wrote: 'I was uncomfortable when he was around and he was uncomfortable with me. I had usurped what he took for granted: an inalienable right to be the centre of attention.'

The most startling of all Reith's double standards was the gulf between his private and public stances on sexual morality. He peremptorily sacked a BBC employee who had the temerity to get divorced. And he insisted that the highest standard of rectitude should be observed by whichever broadcaster was entrusted to read the evening *Epilogue*.

Meanwhile, although he never left his shy, blameless and long-suffering wife, Muriel, he paraded a pageant of impressionable and compliant young women at glittering public functions in London.

His effrontery was both cruel and outrageous. He asked his secretary, Joyce Wilson, to escort him on official engagements and invited her down for weekends at the family home - a vast country estate in Berkshire.

Marista, then aged twelve, recalls being perplexed when her hapless mother wondered aloud where the relationship with Joyce 'was all going to end'.

> I met my father only occasionally as a small child, she wrote. And when I did, he was still being a public figure. My role in life was to support his image and to deliver a perfect performance, which I conspicuously failed to do. I don't think he ever regarded me as a real person. He had a complete lack of empathy with other people's lives – he just couldn't understand how they functioned.
>
> I remember, as a child, just wishing he could be more normal. Aside from the fact that he looked so different [apart from being tall, Reith had the scar of a World War I wound across his face] he also sounded different. He didn't talk like other daddies, he just made pronouncements.
>
> I recall being appalled on one occasion, when I made the mistake of inviting two friends from school to our home. My father addressed them just once – and that was to ask when they were leaving.

You would have thought that his daughter's marriage to psychotherapist Murray Leishman, formerly a Church of Scotland minister, would have pleased Reith but that was not to be so.

For several years, Reith was estranged from Marista because she had committed the sin of wanting to get married. 'It was not so much that Reith detested Murray,' wrote Marista. 'He would have felt the same about any man. As one of our friends observed, "Only the fourth person of the Holy Trinity would have been good enough".'

Although her father arrived, grim-faced and perfunctory, to give Marista away on her wedding day, his antipathy to his son-in-law persisted. Indeed, Reith had no compunction in telling Murray how much he loathed him, at one point even moving him to the top of the 'Hate List' that he was constantly updating and revising.

Charming!

....

THE BIRTH OF THE ABC

The Australian Broadcasting Commission was officially launched by the Prime Minister Joseph Lyons on 1 July 1932, It had been cobbled together by the Australian government as a way to regulate broadcast services, and to ensure the that audiences had reasonable access to a range and high standard of radio services.

Before that Australians relied on licensed wireless broadcasting services operated by the Post-Master-General's Department which in turn took over individually owned radio stations across the continent – a conglomerate which had been known as the Australian Broadcasting Company. It began with a cultural cringe. The first chairman of the ABC, Charles Lloyd Jones, warned his audiences not to expect the standards of the BBC (not that Australians would know anything of what the BBC was doing anyway), as the colonial culture could not compete with the 'high broadcast standards of London'.

It was, however, based on the Reithian BBC model and was originally funded by a combination of licence fees and some government funding.

The early services of the ABC included 12 radio stations across the wide brown land for 11 hours a day.

But it quickly became a fixture of daily life for many Australians.

In establishing the ABC, the government appointed a board of directors with five commissioners, including a chairman and vice-chairman. The board met for the first time on 27 May 1932, but did not appoint the ABC's first General Manager, Major Walter Conder, until the following year and did not advertise the job.

Conder was no Reithian colossus. He was described by ABC historian Ken Inglis as 'a chirpy man-about-town with a showman's flair for broadcasting' who glowed at his success in running Melbourne's 3LO until the Australian Broadcasting Company took it over in 1928.

He was one of the country's first returned soldiers after being hit by Turkish bullets on the initial Gallipoli landing on 25 April 1915. For the rest of the war he had charge of venereally-diseased soldiers in a hospital camp at Langwarrin, near Melbourne, where he helped restore the dignity of these miserable men by such devices as having them take turns in guarding each other and starting a brass band.

He came recommended by the Prime Minister Joe Lyons, who had known him as a young man in Tasmania. For a time after the war he was an overseer in a rubber plantation in Papua, before being made Governor of Victoria's largest prison, Pentridge.

But while he worked well with the first chairman, Sir Charles Lloyd Jones, the ebullient Conder clashed with the second, William James Cleary from July 1934. Conder believed that programs should be arranged to suit the masses. He did not believe in many talk sessions or in controversial broadcasts.

He wanted more sporting programs, more entertainment for its own sake or as he put it 'everything on the air but hot air'. Cleary could not accept either Conder's outlook or his 'barrack-room standards'.

To get rid of him, Cleary alleged irregularities in Conder's expenditure of ABC funds in 1935 but the precise details were never made clear. The commission dismissed Conder but granted compensation equal to one half- year's salary. News of his 'resignation' came as a complete surprise to the public.

(With the aid of his severance money Conder formed a company to run Ivan Brothers' International Circus but the enterprise failed. Possibly a hardly more daunting task than 'herding cats' of volatile ABC broadcasters.)

....

THE MOSES ERA

His successor was Charles Moses, an Englishman who was a graduate from the Sandhurst Royal Military College, saw service in the post-World War I army of occupation in Germany and migrated to Australia in 1922. He invested his army pay-out in his parents' fruit farm, but lost the lot when this venture failed.

After selling real estate, working as a physical training instructor (Moses was superbly fit throughout his long life and an imposing figure over six ft tall [183 centimetres], and worked as a car salesman before the Depression struck. He thought the rapidly growing radio industry might be a better bet, as he had a well-modulated southern English accent which, as ABC historian Neville Petersen later wrote, 'avoided class-based extremes'.

Indeed it was the kind of voice Australian radio stations everywhere thought ideal.

He auditioned with the then Australian Broadcasting Company and some months later was suddenly called in to describe an ice-hockey game.

Moses had never even seen an ice hockey match, but he said he knew all about it, found a manual and boned up on it for two hours and his broadcast was so well received he was asked to join the regular staff!

*Charles Moses faking 'live' broadcasts of test
cricket in 1932 general terms about the game.*

So by July 1932 when company he worked for was amalgamated into the Australian Broadcasting Commission he had a growing reputation as an announcer and news and sports commentator. His knowledge of sport was prodigious and first hand. He represented Victoria in rugby union football, was a champion discus-thrower, had been an amateur heavyweight boxing champion as well as playing soccer, cricket and hockey for good measure.

He became famous during the 'synthetic' supposedly 'live' broadcasts where ball-to-ball descriptions were faked in the studio using gramophone records of applause, descriptions of the play that came in spasmodically by ticker-tape, and ingeniously making up the time between balls, and the next cable, by chatting in general terms about the game. (He created the sound of bat hitting ball by tapping a pencil on various hollow roundels of wood.)

By 1933 Moses was the ABC's sporting editor, federal controller of talks a year later, and by 1935 general manager! He and the chairman, Cleary, got on well and together put together the structure of today's ABC, with its federal departments of talks, drama and music, run by specialists, and fostered Australian talent to create a genuinely national enterprise.

Supported by the conductor Bernard Heinze Moses quickly established state orchestras of professional musicians, augmented by gifted amateurs, bringing in internationally recognised artists and conductors whom he recruited, charmed and entertained during their Australian visits. By the late 1940s, the ABC had five permanent state orchestras, enabling national tours by the visiting celebrities.

The entry of the Japanese into the Pacific war in late 1941 saw Moses leave the ABC and join the AIF as a company commander of the 2/20th Battalion in Singapore. He was hand-picked to join the staff of General Gordon Bennett, the commander of the 8th Division. In the brief action against the invading Japanese he survived two Japanese ambushes. On 15 February, the day of the Allied surrender to the Japanese after the fall of Singapore, he persuaded Bennett that escape was possible and commandeered a sampan in Singapore Harbour and sailed to Sumatra, then part of the Netherlands East Indies still held by the Dutch. His boss, Bennett, was flown to Australia and Moses eventually followed. Bennett's escape was controversial, and he played no further part in the war.

Moses, however, was appointed a lieutenant colonel and in April 1943 temporarily commanded the 2/7th Cavalry Regiment which fought at Sanananda, Papua, where he was mentioned in dispatches. Shortly after that, the Prime Minister John Curtin requested he return to head the ABC

Curtin wanted Moses not only to develop the national broadcaster's national consciousness and culture, but most importantly to develop its own news service – something that Moses had been trying to do since he first became general manager, but had been frustrated by the opposition of the newspaper proprietors.

In February 1945 Charles Moses attended the Empire Broadcasting Conference in London. The war in Europe had not then ended, and the BBC invited the war veteran to observe its reporting of the war there. He saw from close range Field Marshal Bernard Montgomery's attack on Wesel on the Rhine and joined the commandos crossing the river.

He and two companions were lucky to escape injury when German self-propelled guns shelled a factory building in which they were hiding.

The war over, Moses was adept at publicising new activities that drew increasing audiences to the ABC. The newly created Rural Department, with its *Country Hour* kept regional families in touch with marketing trends, farming methods and the latest weather information. The News Department, created in 1947, was now able to broadcast its own radio news service independent of the press. Moses quickly realised the importance of offering an apparently impartial choice of news, and focused on events taking place in Federal and State parliaments.

But by the late 1950s Moses's post-war honeymoon with the press and public opinion began to pall. His claim to have the confidence of both sides of politics was negated in October 1957 when the deputy leader of the Federal Opposition, Arthur Calwell, verbally attacked him in the House.

Calwell described Moses as 'sickening' and 'slimy' because he had deliberately withheld until parliament was in recess the announcement that an Englishman, Peter Homfray, an unsuccessful Liberal Party of Australia candidate for the Tasmanian parliament, had been appointed to the position of director of Radio Australia. Alleging that Moses was preventing Australians from securing promotions within the ABC, Calwell listed other recent senior appointments of Englishmen and declared that, 'I would facilitate his departure to the BBC, where he properly belongs'.

Television was introduced to Australia in 1956, in time for the Melbourne Olympic Games. Moses ensured the ABC was in the forefront of the action by assuring the Commission that he could do it on the cheap, by grafting the new medium on to the existing radio structure. This was somewhat clumsy and difficult to achieve without television professionals who had to be trained. But Moses just powered on. In 1961 producer Robert Raymond and broadcaster Michael Charlton approached Moses for support to produce a new type of program, based on the BBC's *Panorama*, which would deal with contentious social and political issues. The staff in the programs and talks departments at first strongly opposed the idea, believing that the vetting of content would involve too much work.

Moses overruled them and the program *Four Corners* went ahead, with the co-producers reporting to him directly. It still broadcasts to this day.

Moses often acted in secret and on his own initiative, to thwart decisions of his chairman, the commission and the government on matters that he thought were important in terms of principle.

When Prime Minister Sir Robert Menzies banned the showing in 1963 on ABC television of a BBC interview with Georges Bidault – a former prime minister of France and opponent of President Charles de Gaulle – then living in exile, Moses was determined to make the public aware of the government's action.

As the ban did not apply to commercial stations, he rang Sir Frank Packer, chairman of TCN-9, Sydney, and offered him the film on the proviso that he did not disclose its source. To the government's acute embarrassment, TCN-9 showed the interview.

Ever a physical fitness enthusiast, distinguished visitors were on occasions surprised to see their host open a glass case, produce a razor-edged competition axe and demonstrate its sharpness by removing some hair from the arm or leg of whoever had come to see him. (Moses had been introduced to wood-chopping while in Pemberton, Western Australia, in 1944, and had taken it up as his main hobby.) He celebrated his 50th birthday by walking 80 kilometres on that day!

He was still general manager when I began freelance interviewing for the ABC in 1958, and I met him once when he visited the Hobart headquarters of the ABC. I still have his signature on my first ABC pass, certifying my credentials with the national broadcaster. He resigned in January 1965 having been the ABC's general manager for 30 years.

....

ENTER TALBOT DUCKMANTON

Like Charles Moses before him, the ABC's next general manager Talbot Sydney Duckmanton started his broadcasting career as a sporting announcer with the national broadcaster. He spoke in calm, well-modulated tones with that faintly Anglicised accent spoken hardly anywhere in Australia outside broadcasting studios.

(This tradition lasted well into the 1970s when announcers dominated spoken word on the ABC. Arthur Wyndham, a broadcaster who played a key role in the introduction of ABC television in Australia, had similarly orotund tones as long as I knew him. Arthur eventually headed the department who hired announcers.

He issued an instruction that if anyone came for an audition as an ABC announcer and sounded like him, 'he is not to be hired'. Women announcers were as rare as the proverbial hens' teeth in those days.

Duckmanton, who was the son of an architect, joined the ABC as a trainee announcer in 1939 having been auditioned, in his school uniform would you believe, by Charles Moses. During World War II he served as a pilot in the RAAF before becoming an ABC war correspondent in 1945. Then he was a national newsreader and outside broadcast commentator before moving into managerial posts in Queensland and Tasmania.

In the ABC's old headquarters in Hobart, opposite the General Post Office in Macquarie Street, was a creaking old-fashioned lift with a wire grill inner door, presided over by equally venerable lift operator Mr Oliphant. The story goes that when Duckmanton first arrived for work as state manager, Mr Oliphant had not completely mastered his new boss's name. He would open the lift door and say, 'Good morning Mr Manton'. After about three days of this, Duckmanton took his pipe out of his mouth and said, 'Look my name is not Mr Manton, it's Duckmanton, and I'd like you to call me by that name'.

'Oh no, Mr Manton! I couldn't possibly be so familiar.'

In his announcing days he was one of three Commonwealth broadcasters assigned to the BBC team to help describe the Queen's Coronation procession in 1953.

Talbot Duckmanton had none of the convivial charm of his predecessor the ebullient Charles Moses. A shy, balding man, he cultivated an aura of dignity supported by his ever-present pipe, which lived in his mouth. When he needed time to consider what he might say next, he would pull out a little pipe-management tool kit and prod and tamp the contents of the bowl for some unfathomable purpose before responding. When Moses took over the ABC in 1935, he had to administer fewer than 300 people who were employed to get programs out on 14 radio stations. By the time Duckmanton was handed the ABC's reins in 1965 the national broadcaster had 83 radio stations, 24 television stations and a staff of five thousand.

Unlike the publicity prone and flamboyant Moses, Duckmanton (above) had a reserved nature and liked to give the impression of a deep thinker, cautious and discreet who played his cards close to his chest. ABC historian Ken Inglis wrote of him:

> The new general manager smoked a pipe, not cigars [as Moses always did] and drank sparingly. No loyal courtier would hope to please by putting fresh words to *Little Brown Jug*, or singing *Here's a Health unto Sir Talbot*. [Duckmanton was knighted in 1980.] There were no trials of strength at drinking or walking or wood-chopping or

throwing the medicine ball, Duckmanton got his daily exercise and relaxation in the swimming pool at Tattersalls Club [conveniently just around the corner from the ABC's HQ Broadcast House] and went home in the evenings.

Moses had been something of a buccaneer in the way he forged the ABC he controlled for three decades and he had little in common with Duckmanton who succeeded him. In fact the two men could not stand each other. In 1962 Moses had played a key role in creating the Asia-Pacific Broadcasting Union, and a year before he retired had himself appointed as secretary general with the ABU secretariat located in Sydney. Even after he retired in 1965, his long-term secretary Betty Cook remained with him while he continued with his ABU responsibilities.

In 1966, by then based in Singapore, I was relieving the Jakarta correspondent Philip Koch for six weeks while he took some leave, and I learned that Sir Charles Moses was coming there on ABU business.

To my surprise, I was informed that Duckmanton had told the Singapore regional office that no special facilities should be accorded to Moses (although Duckmanton was later president of the ABU that Moses had set up) and that he should not be met at the airport by the ABC car.

I thought about this for about five seconds and decided to disobey orders. I went with the driver to Jakarta airport to meet Moses, who breezed through Indonesian Customs with six bottles of Scotch whisky and his usual bonhomie, and invited me for a drink in his hotel room when we got there.

I thought this was extremely petty behaviour from my general manager, who was renowned for his own love of overseas trips, of which more later.

I worked for the ABC on staff for 30 years, and 17 of them were under the grey eminence of Talbot Duckmanton. Although he, like Moses, believed in hierarchical authority, producers could not be expected to be put on a loose rein as was happening in the BBC under its director general Hugh Carleton Greene. ABC historian Ken Inglis:

Moses had led the ABC like a general, but Duckmanton would be more of a bishop – recognising the partial autonomy of parishes, the existence of diverse tendencies to be accommodated – management, he would say, works these days largely by mediation, not decree.

His stewardship covered a vast extension of the ABC's programming range, notably the introduction of daily radio and television current

affairs programs, the establishment of colour television and the creation of an FM network.

Politically, Duckmanton tended to be a right-winger. Following the Australian Liberal landslide in the 1966 Federal election, Duckmanton officially rebuked ABC's deputy general manager, Clement Semmler, for protesting against Australia's involvement in the Vietnam war, saying, 'You're letting the side down. After all, the ABC has a duty to support the government in this matter'.

Whereas Moses had travelled regularly through the his far-flung ABC empire, meeting staff from managers through to individual broadcasters and support staff, Duckmanton could not bring himself to do this, and led a closeted life with his senior staff in Broadcast House. If he did travel to the state branches he confined his contacts there to upper management. Few staff had ever met him. This was not so, however, in the ABC's overseas offices where Duckmanton seemed to think of himself as a kind of quasi- foreign minister. As a foreign correspondent in Singapore and then New York in the late 1960s I got to know him quite well, as did all the other overseas staff. He asked after our wives and was generally approachable. Because he got to know us, he tended to promote ABC overseas managers to bigger jobs back in Sydney, with varying success, it must be said.

'Wally' Hamilton, one of his assistant general managers, who had built up the ABC News service in his earlier career, was a short man with a bristling moustache, who did not suffer fools gladly. (No one called him Wally or Walter to his face – it was always 'Mr Hamilton'.)

I recall walking with him down Sixth Avenue in New York and struggling for something to say. In some desperation I found myself babbling that New York was a wonderful place to buy classical records, and I had recently bought the entire organ works of J S Bach for $25.

There was a silence while Wally absorbed this information. Eventually he said, 'Yes – Bach was an orderly man'. This seemed to be the last word on the matter, and we continued in silence.

When I arrived in New York from Singapore in mid 1967, the New York manager was Charles Buttrose, an ebullient former close colleague and friend of Charles Moses. Charlie had rejoiced in the dual role of D Pub & Con (ABC jargon for Director of Publicity and Concerts). When Duckmanton took over, he moved the Moses old guard on quickly, and Charlie found himself exiled to New York.

He loved this move actually, as his musical knowledge was encyclopaedic and he was in his element with the big agents in New York like the legendary Sol Hurok, with whom he used to lunch on occasions. He hobnobbed with the famous conductors and soloists of the day to convince them to come and tour in Australia.

Shortly before I arrived, Wally Hamilton had passed through and taken the local staff out to lunch at a good restaurant. Wally's technique with the wine list was to run down the list of the most expensive bottles, and choose something in the mid-range which was always good. His guests could order whatever food they wanted.

So when Duckmanton made his first visit, again before I arrived in mid 1967, Buttrose and the resident correspondent Peter Barnett prepared themselves for a treat. To their bemusement they walked with their new general manager to a nearby Horn and Hardart Automat, a chain of restaurants where sandwiches, hamburgers and prepared food was displayed on shelves behind little glass windows. Customers opened the windows to make their selection, all at economical prices to say the least. Of course there was no liquor licence.

Duckmanton chose a table, and suggested they choose their food. As they chewed on their mass-produced pies or ham sandwiches, washed down with water or Coca Cola, the conversation was stilted. Finally their new general manager said: 'Well, suppose you are wondering why I brought you here'.

They mumbled something inconsequential. Duckmanton went on, 'Well this is a sentimental occasion for me. 'The first time I ever came to New York I was on my own, and I had my first meal in this very Horn and Hardart Automat.' There didn't seem much to say after that, except to look forward to another visit by Walter Hamilton.

For a man obsessed with his own dignity and image, fate had not been kind to him in the naming department. One might have thought that with a surname like Duckmanton his parents had not helped as they looked down at their new-born son in his cradle and decided to christen him Talbot Sydney.

Interviewing people at the airport was all the rage in the early 1970s, and when the British poppy-eyed comedian Marty Feldman made his first visit to Australia, he was interviewed by a reporter, Philip Russell, from the morning radio current affairs program *AM,* who could hardly be prepared for what happened. Here is a transcript of his short interview:

Marty, you are pretty unconventional character. You have bare feet.

That's not unconventional, we are born like that. That's fairly conventional to have bare feet, people just cover them up.

Is there anything that is captured your attention or imagination since you arrived in this country?

Yes, I'm fascinated by Talbot Duckmanton.

Why?

I don't know, it sounds like a village – it's only a small drive to Talbot Duckmanton, or it could be a wine I'll just have a bottle of the Talbot Duckmantons 1953, it could be a lot of things. It could be Talbot and Duckmanton's Favourite Funsters. I think it's a great name. There is also a lovely name in Melbourne, a firm of undertakers called Wood Coffill, and I think W C Fields invented them both.

I think I'd better change the subject. Can you think of some more names or otherwise I might get the sack...

Change it to whatever you like. Let's change the subject. Let's talk about the performance I'm doing at Talbot Duckmanton Theatre in a couple of nights, it's called an evening without Talbot Duckmanton, and it's just an evening of Talbot Duckmantons really.

It's been said that you have a Machiavellian sense of humour, and you're demonstrating that right now.

It's tortuous, I don't know whether it is Machiavellian.

I don't suppose you've had much chance to see anything of Australia yet?

I'd like to see a broken down little mining town, Talbot Duckmanton, which is not far from here and I was hoping to get to it. I was planning to fly Talbot Duckmanton Airlines as a matter of fact, I believe there is a direct flight there.

Mr Feldman...

Duckmanton if you don't mind.

It's terribly difficult to interview you because you seem to come back to this name fixation that you have.

I don't know, I just have a fixation about names. I once invented a name on radio...

What was it, dare I ask?

Oh yes, everyone objected to it and nobody can say why they thought it was offensive. And I'll bet you couldn't tell me. It sounds obscene. 'Gruntfuttock'. Now there is nothing wrong with that name at all, a futtock is part of a ship. And when people complained about it being an obscenity, you had to ask 'what, how', and nobody had an answer. I just like weird names. I like the names Dickens used to invent. Another name,' Pontiscack' was invented by my great friend Spike Milligan. That's a great name.

Now that you're in Australia will you be incorporating any Australian material in your shows?

No, I shall simply do the Talbot Duckmanton medley I suppose, which I normally do.

I think we've sort of run out now really, unless there is anything else you'd like to talk to me about?

I would like to talk to you about Talbot Duckmanton and whether it can be treated privately and confidentially these days. 'I'm sorry, you have a touch of Talbot Duckmantons. There is very little we can do.'

Marty Feldman, back in the UK, would you do something like this to someone in the BBC?

Yes, if someone had a name like that. If I could get it through the customs of course…

The interview never made it to air, so Talbot Duckmanton didn't get to hear it, alas. However bootlegged copies quickly made their way around the ABC traps, and I still have mine.

In the early part of his stewardship of the national broadcaster, Australia had been governed by conservative Liberal governments for 23 years since 1949. It was not until 1972 that Gough Whitlam's Labor government was elected, using the apt and powerful slogan 'It's Time'.

The last two years of the Liberal government under the stewardship of the hapless Prime Minister William McMahon were fearful of the ABC's hard- hitting television current affairs programs, the five days a week *This Day Tonight* and the weekly investigative *Four Corners* documentary current affairs flagship that had been running since 1961. *TDT* used to run satirical segments in its mix, and McMahon's almost daily gaffes were meat and drink to this genre and newspaper cartoonists. The ABC's parent department in those days was the PMG (Postmaster Generals Department) presided over by Sir Alan Hume who saw the ABC current affairs reporters as a nest of lefties, not properly controlled by ABC management or board.

Commenting on the ABC's budget estimates for 1970-71, he proposed in a letter to the chairman of the commission, Sir Robert Madgwick, that cuts be made specifically to the budgets of *Four Corners* and *This Day Tonight*.

ABC staff leaked the letter to the newspapers and, in the subsequent furore over the independence of the ABC, Hulme was forced to retreat but remained unrepentant.

The Labor government only lasted five years and like the Liberals before it was often miffed by what it saw as unfair treatment by the ABC, which took its reputation for independence seriously as it always had. In 1975, the then leader of the opposition, Malcolm Fraser, took the drastic step of threatening to not to pass Labor's appropriation bills in the Senate, which finances federal government operations, potentially starving it of its funding to pay public service salaries and more. On 11 November, Whitlam intended to call a half Senate election to break the deadlock, but Australia's Governor General Sir John Kerr beat him to it earlier that day by taking the unprecedented step of withdrawing Whitlam's commission as prime minister, sacked the government, appointed Malcolm Fraser as acting prime minister. He sacked the Labor government and fresh elections were called. A Liberal government, headed by Malcolm Fraser, was returned a month later.

Conservative Australian governments have always been uneasy about the ABC, and seem to delight in cutting its funding, on which the ABC is completely dependent.

The longest serving Liberal prime minister since Sir Robert Menzies is John Howard. One of his senior advisers, Graeme Morris, once famously said in 1997 of the ABC that it was a case of 'our enemies talking to our friends, on the basis that it was a left-leaning media outfit that broadcast chiefly to a Liberal-voting audience.

By 1978 the Liberals had stacked the ABC board with their own and must have been delighted when the long-running thorn in their side, *This Day Tonight*, was axed by the new ABC board and its replacement, an hour- long combined news and current affairs program called *Nationwide* was moved back from *TDT*'s high rating 7.30 pm slot to the much later 9.30 pm spot.

As it happened, combining straight news with current affairs was an uneasy mix, despite being hosted by the engaging and popular Geraldine Doogue, and was never popular with the ABC's audience. Management tried moving it back to 8.30 pm – and even further to 6.30 pm, straddling the old TV news 7 pm half hour. But the audience clearly wanted their straight news where it had always been, and current affairs went back to the 7.30 pm half-hour slot in 1986, renamed *The 7.30 Report*, first with separate state editions and from 2011 in that timeslot nationally, titled simply *7.30*. At the time of writing it is still going strong four nights a week, compered by Leigh Sales.

However in 1978, particularly in the opinion of its staff, the ABC was in dire straits with heavy staff cuts demanded by the Fraser government, the budget ever-pruned, continuing its steady decline. The ABC found itself unable to bid effectively for rights to televise major sporting events or to show overseas programs. Production of local drama had been reduced, and facilities for getting and presenting news had fallen a long way behind the standards of the commercial stations. The ABC's Commission instructed their chairman John Norgard, to the ABC's minister, Tony Staley, reporting 'that the government was seriously prejudicing the Commission's ability to carry out its basic statutory responsibility… to provide 'adequate and comprehensive' radio programs for the Australian community.

On top of that came that the government's plan to axe the position of staff elected commissioner.

The staff were ropable, particularly when *This Day Tonight* was forbidden by management from interviewing John Croyston, the federal president of the ABC Staff Association, on this development. ABC radio news reported this on next morning's 6.45 am bulletin, but it was censored from later bulletins on the orders of the controller of news Russell Handley. Next day there was no news on radio or television as News journalists went on strike over this intervention.

On 25 October 1978 the current staff elected commissioner Marius Webb joined a thousand or so ABC workers at a stopwork meeting called at Sydney's Regent Theatre by the NSW branch of the Staff Association to protest about the ending of his post and cuts in funding and staff ceilings. This would be the first of three such meetings over the next three weeks, and the prelude to the longest and most serious strike the ABC had ever seen. The first resolution on the agenda was a vote of no confidence in the ABC's board chairman, John Norgard. It was proposed by the long term presenter of ABC radio's *Science Show*, Robyn Williams. Here is part of what he said:

> …I'm sick of being a laughing stock. I'm sick of watching the ABC fall apart. Sick of waiting for one public statement of concern from Mr Norgard, waiting for the smallest, the slightest action from him or indeed from senior management to show that they are doing something to save the ABC.
>
> Let me tell you a little story. Last week my phone rang. I was out. The administrative assistant in Science answered my phone, and as that was the third call she had answered in as many minutes, she was a trifle short. 'Science', she said, 'Can I help you?' 'I'd like to speak to Robyn Williams'. 'Well I'm sorry, he's out of the office. There are no mail boys again and he's gone for the mail.'
>
> 'Oh,' said the man at the other end, and he asked to leave a message. 'Who is it,' she asked'? 'Tell him John Norgard rang'.
>
> Oh yes, Mr Norgard knows all about the conditions in which we work. He knows how one person must now do the work three did before.

He knows that our studios are falling apart. He knows that our best broadcasters are leaving in droves. He knows that there are people in television who been sitting there looking at the wall for months because there is no budget to make programs. He knows that some departments have been rundown so far it will take years for them to be capable of operating effectively again – if at all! He knows these things because we have told him.

So what does Mr Norgard do all this knowledge? How does he feel about resigning over the decline of one of Australia's most important institutions? Well, I don't think Mr Norgard sees himself as part of the ABC at all. The only way to understand his actions is to believe he thinks he is the head of a rival organisation. Then it makes sense. He is the opposition to the ABC.

What other explanation could there be for someone to go public, as he did and say on [the evening radio current affairs program] *PM* that there is no problem with morale in the ABC. And when the Staff Association sent a telegram deploring that statement his reply telegram said: 'There is no problem with morale beyond that caused by staff cuts and budget restrictions'. I mean that's like saying that someone is alive and well from having his head cut off.

The vote of no confidence was carried unanimously.

(I recall one of the television graphics artist did a wonderful cartoon of a spray-can marked *NORGARD – Will only work if shaken vigorously.*)

A staff association delegation asked to see the Minister for Posts and Telecommunications, Tony Staley. He refused to give any indication about future budget and staff cuts to the ABC, or the restoration of the staff elected commissioner. So another general stopwork meeting was organised in Sydney on 9 November.

It says something about the difficulty of sacking public servants in those days, that I volunteered to propose a vote of no confidence in my ultimate boss Talbot Duckmanton and speak to it. (My background was in news and current affairs, but I was working at the time as a producer for the Department of Radio Drama & Features in Sydney.) Here is part of what I said:

I have worked with the ABC now for some 15 years in a state branch in television and radio and I've been an overseas correspondent. Now because of that last one, I've met the general manager. Not many staff have, but if you are overseas with the ABC you meet him a lot.

Because the general manager does a lot of overseas travelling. I'm not saying this is improper – we don't want to be insular, but Mr Duckmanton really makes a meal of it.

Now when that jumbo jet lifts off from Mascot, Mr Duckmanton becomes a different man. Not long after he hears the musical rumble of the duty-free trolley trundling down the aisle, he becomes affable, approachable and extraordinarily friendly with ABC staff. It is no coincidence that many of his senior appointments in the past have been made from overseas staff, because they are the ones he's actually had time to talk to and get to know. And we are all aware of those courtesy sweetheart deals that are made with certain overseas staff to keep them in their perk filled hideaways – for more than a decade in some cases.

But meeting in the foyer of Broadcast House when he's making that awkward dash between the lifts and Tattersalls club – where he actually might have to see or talk to ABC staff – and you'd think an ancient flathead been waved under his nose.

Yes, Mr Duckmanton is very heavily addicted to overseas travel. It seemed, as a colleague said,' he'd become hooked on smallpox inoculations and cholera jabs'. It must be a great relief to leave the ABC's scan of worms behind and jet off on the international circuit. It's hardly a coincidence today, when we staffers are meeting to worry and agonise over the very future existence of the ABC, the general manager is – surprise, surprise – overseas at an international broadcasting conference. In Mauritius this time.

People will often say, 'Ah yes, Tal Duckmantont is a shy man, not good at the fronting bit, but he works very effectively behind the scenes. He's got a brilliant mind and great administrative ability'. Now over the years I really wanted to believe this. Maybe it's all true. But no Mr Duckmanton, you are tired, possibly even bored, and certainly not the man to lead the ABC these critical times.

The ABC needs a new Pope… a new general manager. How about Polish one? We really need to see some results.

A colleague of mine put it better I think when he described Talbot Duckmanton as having a great wrestling brain – but no arms. That he would, at times, give a brilliant summation to a senior ABC conference, on problems facing the organisation, politically, financially and administratively.

But when someone asked, 'What are you going to do about it?', his arms visibly retracted into his torso.

The stopwork meeting also resolved to prevent the broadcasting of the national parliament, until the staff-elected commissioner's position was re-instated. ABC historian Ken Inglis later wrote:

On Wednesday 15 November, Lionel Barr, an operations officer in the [radio] switchroom at Forbes Street who had worked tranquilly for the ABC since 1964, was directed by his superiors in the Engineering Division to put parliament on the air, and by his comrades in the Staff Association to keep it off. At 2.13 pm he pulled the plug. When Barr was stood down, members of the ABC Staff Association and the Australian Journalists Association went on strike, followed by members of the Musicians Union.

Day after day people in New South Wales and Canberra could see nothing on ABC television but a milky glow and hear nothing on ABC radio. 'How does explain the intricacies of industrial action to a two- and-a-half-year-old?' a parent wrote to the *Sydney Morning Herald*. 'Daddy, can I watch *Big Bird* on *Sesame Street*'? '*Big Bird*'s on strike dear'.

For many grown-ups the deprivation of radio was harder to endure. During its absence, Maurice Dunleavy wrote in the *Canberra Times* that the strike had taught him 'that the ABC is the most pervasive, most important and most varied force in culture and current affairs in this country.

On 19 November, our absent general manager, Talbot Duckmanton, jetted back into Mascot Airport from Mauritius. I was part of a striking staff delegation that met him at the airport. We decided not to say anything, just stand silently with our placards as he walked past us, which he did without looking left or right. WELCOME HOME TAL, was the headline in the *Strike News*. But he remained missing in action. It seemed Duckmanton was ill and went into hospital, while his deputy, Graham White who had been acting for him, was left to try to sort out the mess.

The strike ended two days later. Lionel Barr would be reinstated without penalty, and all bans on transmission, including parliament, would be lifted.

Not a lot had been achieved. The issue of the staff elected commissioner was not pressed, and no further negotiations promised.

DID YOU MISS THE ABC? asked the Friends of the ABC in an advertisement paid for by the reclusive author Patrick White and nearly 300 other people.

So did the ABC staff, who lost more than $350,000 in wages during the strike. 1600 commission staff were prepared to forfeit a week's wages to alert the public to the dangerously run-down condition of the national broadcaster.

In 1982, Duckmanton decided he would retire at the age of 61. He would be the first general manager of the ABC to retire on his own terms. He had been the fourth general manager in the Australian Broadcasting Commission's 50 years of existence. The first acting general manager, H P Williams, a former rural journalist, died in 1933 in the saddle during the first year he was appointed. Major Conder, the first confirmed general manager was fired in 1935, Moses had been shown the door on his 65th birthday with what he thought was indecent haste and Duckmanton decided to take his leave in the closing stages of the Australian Broadcasting Commission in 1982 (before it became a Corporation). This ensured he would be there for the ABC's 50th birthday for which he had worked since the organisation was six years old, after having been taken on the staff by Charles Moses at the age of 17.

He had been GM for seventeen years. He and Moses had spanned 47 years at the helm of the national broadcaster. No general manager (soon to be managing director) since 1982 would ever again serve more than two five year terms.

7.

AUNTY LIFTS HER SKIRTS

Who is 'Aunty' ABC?

Aunty is an independent-minded woman in her sixties who lives in the Dandenongs, wears a parka and inclines towards eating what we weren't meant to eat and believing what we weren't meant to believe.

G James, North Carlton, Vic

In August 1982, the fifth (and last) general manager of the ABC was appointed from within. Keith Jennings, who had been Assistant General Manager for Management Services had only been with the national broadcaster for two years and was GM for only 18 months before resigning to take up a job as an academic administrator.

The ABC became the Australian Broadcasting Corporation in 1983, and its first managing director, Englishman Geoffrey Whitehead, was appointed on 23 January 1984. Few people had ever heard of him. He had been a journalist with Reuters in London and a political correspondent with the BBC. He came to the ABC from his current job as Director General of Radio New Zealand – and had become a New Zealand citizen. He lasted for three years, before bizarrely being replaced by the chairman of the ABC Board, David Hill! But more of that in a moment.

I am grateful to Geoffrey Whitehead for a suggestion he made about a new television program, which was to involve me. Apparently BBC-TV has a program called *Points of View*, a weekly session which allow viewers to write in and say what they think about the various programs they had seen. Now my entire career in the ABC up to late 1985 had been in radio, so I was surprised to be visited one morning in my office at the ABC's Social History Unit by Peggy McDonald, then head of the ABC's Audience Research Unit. She mentioned that Whitehead had asked her to explore doing something similar to *Points of View* with the ABC, and she and others had thought of me as a presenter.

I thought there must be some mistake, and said so – I considered my middle-aged rather crumpled face was far better suited to radio. Television and I had been uneasy bedfellows. On the few occasions I had done studio interviews for *This Day Tonight* (because no one better was available), the results had not been encouraging.

Radio interviewers use their faces and bodies a lot to encourage people to talk, rather than muttering 'ah ha', or 'um-goodness me', or giggle or other things which would make later sound editing difficult. Television interviewers have to sit like graven images by comparison. On my few TV live appearances, every time the director cut to me, I was invariably grimacing or jumping about like a cane toad about to be it by a No 7 iron.

The more I thought about the likelihood of the camera switching to me, the more nervous I became. The more tense I grew the more one side of my mouth closed up as though afflicted by a partial stroke. I was happiest away from studio cameras.

Peg was an emissary from the ABC's then Controller of Television, Paddy Conroy. I said, 'Why me?'

'Because we think you can write a witty script.'

'Thanks for saying that, but there must be another reason.'

Peg paused, and said almost defiantly, 'We like your strong larrikin streak'.

'I think that is the nicest thing senior management has said about me for years!'

Peg thought I should give it a go. I was not allowed to see a broadcast of the BBC's *Points of View* and we didn't have a name. I wanted to go with *Dear Aunty* but the all-powerful Paddy Conroy didn't like it. We had a week to come up with something better. *Backchat* leapt out of the pages of *Roget's Thesaurus* to head the short list. It seemed appropriately short, pungent and cheeky.

It wasn't until we had been on air for about two months that we discovered it was also the name of a regular column in Adelaide's *The Advertiser* and a number of published newsletters, including the *Border Collie Club of Victoria*, the *Back Pain Research Foundation of Western Australia* and the *Australian Ankylosing Spondylitis Society of Victoria*. Mercifully there is no copyright in titles.

The plan was for me to introduce letters from listeners and viewers (soon to include faxes and recorded telephone calls in those pre-internet days) and provide appropriate responses. ABC consumers could write in about radio too, but television dominated the 10 minutes twice a week, on Tuesdays and Thursdays at 9.25 pm. Peg McDonald retired from her Audience Research job, and took on the important but often tiresome task of sifting through the letters, removing the dross and sorting them into topics.

(She did this for the next nine-and-a-half-years!) I worked through the weekend to prepare two scripts, which were pre-recorded at the rather ungodly hour of 7 am on Tuesday mornings).

I practised not twitching and jumping about on camera, and we went to air for the first time on 28 January 1986. I noted that *Backchat*'s first producer Ron Elliott found it hard to find a diplomatic description for the *Sydney Morning Herald*'s television reviewer of the compere he had to put on camera. 'Tim is one of the real people – not super pretty!'

Jim Oram, television critic on *The Daily Telegraph* Sydney thought so too, and wrote:

had　nel 10 execu... ..
ous　　Backchat's format is
ras　astonishingly simple. Its
by　commentator, Tim Bow-
den, who reminds one of
life　a koala and therefore
ght　should be protected, sits
ers　in front of a camera in-
ise　troducing written com-
it-　ments from viewers.
or　　Being the ABC, the let-
t-　ters tend to verge on the
esoteric, pointing out,
say, that a figurine de-
scribed in a drama series
as from the Sung Dy-
nasty was in fact from
the T'ang.
　　Feminism often rais
querulous head.
social beh-
was ever
ast w
r

Viewers quickly perceived that *Back-Chat* was their place for letters of complaint, praise, suggestions or questions on programs and policies.

Although only a small percentage of letters received could ever get to air, we had a policy of replying to every letter that came in. We didn't have to make any up (as one correspondent cheekily suggested) as there were always plenty to choose from. And we didn't broadcast anonymous letters, or indeed *noms de plume*. I remarked on air that I had grave doubts about the veracity of one surname because there weren't any other Frizzletits in the phone book.

Mavis wrote back in alleged distress because I had made fun of her name.

Having verified that she was a real person, Mavis became a regular contributor. She had a particular penchant for raunchy and tasteless excerpts from ABC programs, which naturally gave us the opportunity to run them again so people who had missed them could get an eye and earful.

Mavis Frizzletit, I found out, was a psychiatric nurse by profession. I did invite her on to *BackChat* in person for an end of year special program and she appeared back-lit, to preserve her anonymity. She actually broke up the Control Room with her first answer – which is hard to do with those case-hardened professionals:

> Me: Now Mavis, I want to ask you about your name. I have looked in the Sydney phone book, and there are NO Frizzletits listed, none.

> Mavis: Actually Tim there are hundreds there. You see Frizzletit is Gaelic for 'Smith'.

Recording had to pause while not only the Control Room lads but I struggled to regain composure. And, of course, her real name was Smith.

Letters of praise and thanks to the ABC for what it did got occasional mention, but the very nature of *BackChat* meant that the more inventive the invective in the correspondence, the greater chance there was of making it to air. *Thou shalt not bore* is one of the cardinal rules of radio and television and we tried to maintain it.

One of our earliest correspondents was Mary Forbes, or Cremorne, New South Wales. It emerged in one of her letters that she was over 80.

Regrettably, I put 'older voice over' in the script. (The voices were all done by ABC television staff in their spare time, and they weren't paid.)

However Mary was far from pleased. 'Dear Mr Bowden, I may be over eighty, but I do not have a cracked voice... please in future do let any future correspondence re read as though I was the Witch of Endore',

As the years went on, we started to run some BackChat Christmas specials. One I recall, involved Gary Sweet. But the call sheet, as we refer to them, had an unexpected element...

Backchat

SCHEDULE:

1230 hrs	Camera & Sound Crew to Meet Des Murphy & Angela Blasonato in ABC TV Foyer, Gore Hill to travel to location. Loc: Barcoo Studios 32 Barcoo Street East Roseville
1300 hrs	Set Up for Interview. Loc of Interview TBA. on Day.
1330	Angela will meet Gary in Make Up.
1345-1430	Record Interview with Gary Sweet & Tim.
1445-1530	Prick Ups with Tim
1600	Wrap

Funny, I have no memory of those!

Certainly our consumers did not pull their punches. Andrew Denton was one of the ABC's most innovative and entertaining producers and presenters. His comedy/talk show *The Money Or The Gun* ran from 1989- 1994.

Not everybody liked it, including Ian Morrison, of Frankston, Victoria:

C standing for crudworthy
R rubbish,
A for anal,
P for pathetic,
U for undescribable,
L for lunatic,
O for offensive,
U for unbearable and
S for proverbial sewerage.

Now I mentioned that the new managing director Geoffey Whitehead suggested the concept of *BackChat* which coincided with David Hill's appointment as chairman of the ABC Board. Hill (and his twin brother) had been Fairbridge boys who, although not orphans, came to Australia from England to work on farms in Australia. This was a tough call, and in later years Hill authored a book describing the sexual and other physical abuse perpetrated on tens of thousands of poor or orphaned children sent from former British colonies last century to various institutions.

Geoffrey Whitehead resigned as managing director of the ABC in 1986, and David Hill, who had decided he liked the idea of actually running the ABC rather than the Board, resigned as the Board's chairman and took on the job of managing director.

In 1980 the NSW Labor Premier Neville Wran had appointed Hill as chief executive of the newly formed State Rail authority, charged with making the moribund system more efficient. And by God, he quickly had the trains running on time!

Treading on toes did not worry him, despite being told by one of Wran's ministers to 'pull his head in', and being sledged by an unnamed colleague as 'a cantankerous ego-maniac'. 'A toecutter,' said one unionist. 'Doesn't understand industrial relations' said another, who nevertheless acknowledged his strength of character and charm.

Staff at the national broadcaster cautiously welcomed his appointment. ABC historian Ken Inglis quoted me: 'Tim Bowden of Radio National's Social History Unit and television's *BackChat* hailed Hill as someone used to 'cutting through the bullshit of a large bureaucracy'. He sure was. One of the moves he made early on was to make sure he could sack anyone in the ABC he wanted to.

Although there was a Federal Labour Government when Hill became the ABC's managing director, 'the world's greatest treasurer', as Prime Minister Bob Hawke once called Paul Keating, was not overly generous to the ABC and the Hawke administration was often as irritated as the Conservatives had been by the ABC's tough questioning of its leaders about its policies.

Hill's former closeness to the NSW State Premier Neville Wran cut no ice in Canberra. Treasurer Keating even tightened up the rules on the ABC's budget, increasing the taxes the national broadcaster had to pay, although he was never quite as punitive as the Liberals had been.

Larry Pickering's cartoon in the *Bulletin* magazine in September 1984 gives some indication of Keating's feelings about the national broadcaster.

After Hill became managing director of the ABC, the Commonwealth Public Service was not a safe haven any more – at least for the national broadcaster. It would have been a brave and foolhardy soul who proposed a vote of no confidence in Hill at a union meeting as I had with Duckmanton. I would have been out on my ear in seconds – as I was to experience later when I fell foul of the egocentric but undoubtedly talented human bulldozer David Hill, for a trivial reason.

Being a member of the permanent staff I was delighted to be able to do *BackChat* on my own time, mostly evenings and weekends. The contract was not over-generous but, hey, on top of a public service salary last century, every little helped.

In 1990 we produced *The BackChat Book* featuring some of the more pungent and witty quotes from listeners, illustrated by cartoons from our in house press artists, including John Paice and Verdun Morcombe. In those days the ABC was starting up shops in major shopping centres, and I was invited to attend the opening of the Chatswood ABC shop, in the company of my managing director David Hill.

It was all very cheerful, and I was greeted by ABC aficionados wanting me to autograph *The BackChat Book* as well as other titles I had written, published by ABC Books.

David Hill walked up to me and said, 'You know Tim, you are more popular and well known around here than I am'. A slight chill ran down my spine, as well it might. However the years rolled on and *BackChat* actually did quite well in the ratings, which wasn't bad for two 10 minute programs a week.

In 1994, *Backchat*, fronted by me, had been running for nearly nine years. I decided to take early retirement from the ABC at the ripe old age of 56.

There was not any more stomach by the ABC for the long-form radio oral history-based documentaries I used to do, and the sweet sniff of redundancy was in the air. I had books I still wanted to write and other plans, so decided to take it. However I asked my immediate *BackChat* boss, the head of the ABC's Continuity Department, Patrick Furlong, if I could still do *BackChat*.

He thought I could. My contract had always been on top of my public service salary anyway, and I had just signed up for another two years.

I didn't think this would be a matter of interest to anyone outside the ABC, but I was wrong.

The Sydney Morning Herald at that time used to run a media supplement once a week (it was published on pink paper for some reason) and I think

run by the Melbourne *Age* but coloured blue down south – and one of its columnists rang out of the blue one morning, and she said, 'Is it true you are taking redundancy from the ABC?' I didn't think this was a trade secret, so I said 'Yes'. She went on, 'And will you still be doing *BackChat*'? Again, I said 'Yes', not seeing any great problem with that. She thanked me and hung up.

She then wrote a piece for her column, which gave the impression that I was double-dipping while taking my superannuation. David Hill happened to be overseas at the time, but always had any press clippings about the ABC forwarded to him. He read this. went ballistic and phoned the Controller of Television Paddy Conroy and told him to get rid of me.

Paddy Conroy, the 'Father' of BackChat...

Ironically, Conroy, who existed basically to do what David Hill told him to, had liked to project himself as 'The Father of *BackChat*' as he was involved in its birth in 1986. In the Foreword to *The Backchat Book* in 1990 he said as much, and concluded:

Throughout the last five years of *BackChat*'s life Tim Bowden has maintained his good humour and above all his judgment in the delicate task of being the messenger, carrying as he does both good and bad news.

As yet I don't think anyone wants to shoot the messenger. Long live *BackChat*!

Oh yeah? Briefly, I was paraded before the Father of *BackChat*, Conroy, and shot on Hill's orders. There was a school of thought in the ABC that Hill really enjoyed firing people. My immediate boss, Patrick Furlong, took me to lunch to confirm the bad news. I had just signed a two-year contract, which literally wasn't worth the paper it was written on. As a member of staff when it was drawn up, I had little bargaining power. Effectively the contract said, 'We will pay you if you turn up to present the program, and if you don't, we won't.' I asked Patrick how much of the two years they were going to pay me out. He said, with some embarrassment, 'Three months'. I said that if they wanted me to go graciously (which they did) they would have to do better than that. They offered six months which I accepted and departed, well, graciously. The program was moved to Queensland, and then South Australia and within two years died in the bum.

A year later the storm clouds were gathering over Hill's own tenure, as he had alienated the ABC Board by his bull-at-a-gate crash-through style. I was by then no longer with the ABC, but naturally watched these developments with more than average interest (and it has to be admitted, with some relish) after what I thought was my shabby treatment. He even tried to conceal his own involvement in firing me by hiding behind the skirts of Aunty's Director of Television, his yes man, Conroy. Hell hath no fury like a compere scorned.

On 30 April 1996 the Melbourne *Age* ran this John Spooner cartoon with the apt heading: OVER THE HILL

Those who live by the sword, die by the sword. Goodness me, how sad, never mind.

David Hill and I met briefly at an ABC function some four years after Hill himself had lost the confidence of the Board and resigned – the same situation he had confronted Geoffrey Whitehead with when Hill rolled him when he was Chairman of the Board. I was not surprised to hear him say that he could not remember firing me from *BackChat*!

Just before I exited from my *BackChat* chair I happened to be in makeup at the ABC'S Gore Hill studios in Artarmon, New South Wales, when I coincided with Don Lane, a veteran American performer on Australian television screens since 1969, alternating his versatile talents with stints in his native United States. The *Don Lane Show* was his most enduring Australian program. However he was no shrinking violet and coped with the inevitable ups and downs that abound in this volatile industry.

I didn't know Don all that well, but we knew about each other. He asked me how I was going, and I said, 'Well not all that well Don, David Hill has just fired me from *BackChat*. His response was classic Lane:

'Tim,' he boomed cheerily, 'In television one door closes – and the next slams shut in your face!' He would certainly know, and I cheered up immediately.

After nine years of fronting a twice-a-week television program, I wasn't too distressed to have the manner of my leaving decided for me – although it is better to do it on your own terms if you can.

I am now a fledgling octogenarian (like early *BackChat* correspondent Mary Forbes), and play Scrabble regularly on Facebook with Mavis Frizzletit who is still flourishing, feisty as ever.

FOOTNOTE: *Points of View*, the BBC program that inspired *BackChat* is still on air. The ABC has no similar viewer reaction program to this day.

8

MAKES YOU PROUD TO BE AUSTRALIAN

I have long treasured Michael Leunig's wonderful cartoon to celebrate Australia Day 1984. Where else but Orstraylia? [English pronunciation].

We do have Barry Humphries to thank for spreading the Australian vernacular to the Old Country in the early 1960s – and indeed beyond. His creation of Barry McKenzie, the gormless Aussie making the pilgrimage to England as we did then, has been celebrated in comic strip form in the satirical magazine *Private Eye*, illustrated by Nicholas Garland (later published in three books), and two films directed by Bruce Beresford, during which Bazza attempts to take the piss out of the Poms, with spirited riffs like this:

I hope your chooks turn to Emus
And kick your dunny down flat to the grass.
I hope your balls turn to bicycle wheels
nd back-peddle up your arse.
I hope every lah-di- dah Pommy like you
Gets the trots when he swallows a plum.
Go stick your left eye in hot cocky shit
And your head up a dead bear's bum.

Having lived in London myself in the early 1960s I was well aware of Barry Humphries' contribution to the Australian vernacular through the *Private Eye* comic strips, and his take in Australia skewering the stifling middle- class suburbia of Melbourne and, by inference, elsewhere else.

In 2017 I was invited to explore this phenomenon for *Oz Words*, the journal published by The Australian National University and Oxford University Press, and here it is:

BARRY HUMPHRIES SATIRIST OF SUBURBIA

Growing up in Hobart in the 1950s at the height of Prime Minister Robert Menzies' long reign can be described as comfortable enough, but not very exciting. But despite Menzies exhortation that we were 'British to the bootstraps', we knew we weren't.

Immediate relief was provided by the advent of a young Barry Humphries' tilts at Melbourne's staid and stultifying suburbia ('where the cream brick veneers stay hygienic for years') which came to us in Taswegia in the form of two long playing prized small vinyl records, played at 33 ½ rpm on our parents' turntables. I still have them.

Titled *Wild Life in Suburbia*, these disks introduced us to Edna Everage, and the moribund monotone of Sandy Stone. The back cover, written by Robin Boyd (noted Australian architect and author of *The Great Australian Ugliness*), described the audio treasures awaiting:

Barry Humphries is one of the funniest men you could find this side of hysteria. If this record presented only the funniness of his cracked, elastic voice, there'd be no cause for alarm. But he is also a satirist of Australiana who cuts too close to the awful truth to be considered simply funny. He has us taped in killing caricature, our accent, intonation, vocabulary ('I had a bit of strife parking the vehicle'), the shattered syntax, the activities, accessories, diet – and through it all the ghastly proprieties, the crazy clumsy genteelness of brick-area suburbia.

(The record was marked: FOR DOMESTIC CONSUMPTION ONLY. NOT TO BE EXPORTED ON ANY ACCOUNT.)

Like many Australians of my generation, I headed off to England on the mass transportation of the time, an ocean liner.

In 1960 I arrived in London, where most expatriate Australians clustered in the suburb of Earls Court (I didn't) having sourced reliable supplies of cold, sparkling Fosters ale – a welcome alternative to the warm, flat camel's piss the Poms called beer.

Australians were barely tolerated by Londoners in those days, when Englishmen still wore bowler hats to work. I recall a couple of jokes that illustrate this ambivalence:

A newly arrived Australian thought he saw a mate of his on the other side of the Strand, and raced across the road, slapped him between the shoulder blades (he wasn't wearing a bowler hat), and shouted 'Gudday you old bastard'! An affronted Englishman turned around to investigate this assault. The Australian said, 'Geez mate, I'm sorry. You see in Australia we call our friends bastards'. The Englishman looked him up and down and said, 'And why not?'

On another occasion in the Strand – Australia House was nearby – an Aussie stopped a bowler-hatted businessman and said, 'Excuse me mate, could you tell me where I can take a leak?' The Englishman said, 'Of course. If you walk down to the next street and turn left, you will see a public convenience, and a sign marked "Gentleman". Don't be deterred – walk straight in'.

Barry Humphries was also in London, understudying actor Ron Moody in the role of Fagin in the musical *Oliver*. He did this for several years, during which time Moody NEVER took a sickie, doubtless well aware that Humphries' ferocious talent might rob him of the role. Barry never did play Fagin. I did not live in Earl's Court, nor did Humphries, but in 1961 I managed to interview him for the BBC's Pacific Service, and the ABC's weekly magazine radio program *Scope*. He asked me if I knew any Australians living in Earls Court, and I took him to meet 'a couple of young Australian lasses' who were sharing a flat there. Barry chatted amiably with them, and I could sense him sucking up their idioms and speech patterns like a supercharged vacuum cleaner.

By 1963 I was back in Australia, and Barry was busy making Edna Everage a superstar, improbably both in London and eventually New York!

He also connived with the illustrator Nicholas Garland to produce a monthly comic strip for *Oz Magazine* relating the scatological adventures of Barry McKenzie, a naïve Australian just arrived in London. These were compiled into three paperbacks and published by Sun Books (appropriately in Melbourne), *The Wonderful World of Barry McKenzie* (1968), *Bazza Pulls It Off – More Adventures of Barry McKenzie* (1971) and finally *Bazza Comes Into His Own* (1979).

Bazza's main preoccupations in the course of his bizarre adventures were to get pissed on tubes of ice-cold Fosters whenever possible, and get a root. He succeeded admirably in the first but failed totally in the latter.

It is my belief, that the inventive mind of Barry Humphries made up a great deal of the ocker expressions in these books, some of which have now become part of the Australian lexicon. As micturition is a constant pre-occupation of the beer-swilling Bazza, I suspect that his need to 'point Percy at the porcelain' is one of these. In the interests of scatological scholarship, I have trawled through all three of the above books to suggest which of Bazza's colourful phrases might be Humphries engendered, as well as picking up on older traditional sayings like 'flat out like a lizard drinking'.

I have put an asterisk beside what I think may be Humphries' contributions to the rich vernacular of Australiana, and perhaps *Oz Words* readers may like to comment further. So here we go:

The Wonderful World of Barry McKenzie

*All that Fosters has gone straight to the old feller – am I busting for a nice long snakes...

*I was desirous to choke a darkie

*As fast as a tin of worms with an outboard motor

*Some of the fellers went blind punishing Percy in the palm

*I'd be stiff cracking a fat in mixed company

The kind of sheilah that went off like an alarm clock

*She looks as shifty as a shithouse rat

*To negotiate a coo-ee up the old snake gully (have sex)

*Kevin? Sounds like a flamin' freckle puncher

Bazza Pulls It Off – More Adventures of Barry McKenzie

*Point Percy at the Potables

*Drain the dragon

*I'm as dry as a nun's nasty

I could be up that like a rat up a drain

*Nip into the dunny and siphon the python

*Strain the potatoes

*He's up shit creek in a barbed wire canoe without a paddle

*Built like a brick shithouse

*A bloke like me risks going blind jerkin' the gherkin

*The throttlin' pit (toilet)

I want a girl that goes off like an alarm clock

*Exercise the ferret (have sex)

*Don't come the uncooked crustacean with me (variation on the raw prawn)

Flat out like a lizard drinking...

*Flop your freckle on the grass (sit down)

*You're not going to see my beef bayonet in action (have sex)

*I might have to cry Ruth any second (vomit)

*The Pope's a Jew if that Jam Tart doesn't root like a rattlesnake

*Once she's down to her birthday suit I'll be working her like a belt-fed mortar

I'm that parched I could drink out of a Chinese wrestlers jockstrap

*Choking a darkie (on the toilet)

She's not worth a snatch full of cold water

*Twang the wire (masturbate)

*He's had more sheilahs than you've had spaghetti breakfasts

*Time to splash the boots (urinate)

Go where all the big nobs hang out (visit the urinal)

*I've gotta wring the rattlesnake (same)

I've got to make do with Mrs Palm and her five daughters (masturbate)

*He's that mean he wouldn't give you a sniff of his fart

As lonely as a bastard on Father's Day

All over the place like a mad woman's shit

Smells like someone opened their lunch (fart)

*As cold as a nun's nasty

*As dry as a kookaburra's Khyber

Just shooting through to the gents to shake hands with the unemployed

Bazza Comes Into His Own

*I'll bet she goes off like a tin of bad fish

I hope your balls turn to bicycle wheels and back-pedal up your arse

*If you're that smart you could sell soap to the Poms

I could pull you on like a Wellington boot

You're a flamin' French letter on the prick of progress.

*I'm as dry as Nullarbor Nellie's knickers

*I wouldn't put it up there if the prize was a cooked crayfish and a spare set of balls

As full as a Catholic school

All over the place like a mad moll at a plonk party

She'd bang like a shithouse door in a gale

Dry as a dead dingo's donger

Red sails in the sunset, or, to have the painters in (that time of the month)

*Date with a fur doughnut (self-explanatory)

*Gnawing the 'nana, or, blowing the beef bugle (use your imagination)

*Make love to the lav (to chunder)

....

THE ANGUISH OF BEING BRUCE

Before we leave the wonderful world of Barry Humphries, he is personally responsible for making the lives of all Australian men named 'Bruce' miserable for all time, after suggesting 'Bruce' to the Monty Python team for a sketch satirising Australians. (Humphries nearly offered 'Kevin' instead – I understand Wayne was waiting in the wings) but Barry went for 'Bruce'.)

The late Australian journalist Bruce Wilson had a very compelling reason to write a article on this phenomenon for the Qantas magazine, *The Australian Way*. He first encountered the Bruce factor in London in 1971. Here is part of what he wrote:

At that time I thought that being called Bruce was fairly normal, in the same way that many girls were called Noreen or Raylene or such. It is true that at my high school we had so many boys called Bruce that we all either to have nicknames or be called by a surname simply to distinguish one from the other, but it hardly seems funny.

Dogs were called Spot, cows were called Daisy and boys were called Bruce.

The reason in 1971 that Bruce was so funny in England was that Monty Python did the famous 'Bruce' sketch involving the Department of Philosophy at the University of Woolloomooloo. In that institute of learning, all wore khaki shirts and shorts, had hats with corks bobbing around the edge and were called Bruce. It was only much later than either that the villain of the piece was Barry Humphries, who when asked by the Pythons for a very Ocker name, supplied them with Bruce.

Of course it all died down and I went through brief visits to England in 1974 and 1976 with no Bruce backlash at all. It was then all the more stinging to return in 1977 to find that the Bruce reaction was alive and thriving. They were 'G'day Bruce' ing me all over the country, and I soon ran it to ground. The bloody BBC just rerun the Monty Python series and there was a total resurgence of the joke with the Poms.

Sooner or later even the mightiest of patiences must crack and this happened in the pleasant English Channel port of Hythe, where I spent an idyllic day playing cricket for a local club as its guest. I had top scored – it was very weak bowling and worse fieldling – but as I went off, expecting some polite applause, the incoming batsman said to me in rich Kentish tones, 'Used up all our bleeding luck, haven't you BRUCE'. He hissed the name and went off chortling.

That night, the very civil captain of the team, an ex-Royal Navy commander, had me back to his home for drinks. We watched a dazzling sunset over the sherry and whisky until a very small man came up to me, was introduced, sniggered and said, 'G'day Bruce'.

'What did you say?' I snarled. He was, remember, very small. 'Listen you,' I said, 'do you know the origin of that name? Do you? Are you aware that it is Celtic, Scottish in fact, that it means brave, as in Robert the Bruce, and that people like me and my ancestors have been crossing the English border for centuries and, putting pipsqueaks like you to the sword.'

'Hem', he said. 'Aha, well now. Who would have thought it? Gracious me. Is that so?' The ex-Royal Navy man led me away muttering, 'There, there', and gave me a calming draft as I wiled away the evening giving what I hoped were ferocious Highland glares. As I was leaving. my host said 'Wonderful to see you. But tell me. Just why are so many Australians called Bruce?

It's a good question and I have tried to find the answer.

All of those Bruces with whom I was at school were born between 1940 and 1943 as were many other Australian Bruces I have since met. No one has supplied a good reason. When there is a glut of little boys call Elvis or girls called Lisa, the reason is obvious. Bruce? The only film star of the relevant period I can recall was Bruce Bennett, but his sole claim to fame is a brief stint as Tarzan. After that he made a series of totally forgettable movies, usually playing the heavy. My mother once said, in her vague way, that she thought I was meant to be Peter but since that was the name of her sister's dog confusion would arise, and she settled on Bruce. I wondered why the dog was not called Spot.

There was a time it is true when I used any excuse to go to Scotland where no one ever understood the Monty Python sketch and in Edinburgh and Inverness not an eyebrow twitched when 'Bruce Wilson' was introduced. They simply asked if I was one of the Paisley Wilsons the Gunn clan or of the Border Wilsons or linked with the Mackays. Being a Bruce, it seemed more likely to be of the Paisley family, and there would ensure a long argument fed upon single malt whisky. Either seemed better than being a Python Wilson linked with the Humphries of Melbourne Grammar School.

Now course being an Oz in London is not so bad. We have become cultural, and people gush about our films, our art, even our TV for God's sake. They watched *The Sullivans* and found meaning in it and to it. I like to point out that one of the leading directors is Bruce Beresford. 'Oh yes', they say, 'Beresford, wonderful realism, almost impressionistic primitive lighting, those skies, those set-piece scenes. The wonderful stillness of his camera.'

Ah, yes. Beresford. Not you will notice, poor bloody Bruce.

....

HOW PORT LINCOLN KILLS ITS GALAHS...

This front page picture appeared in *The Adelaide Advertiser* on 22 January 1998.

FATAL BLOW: A split second away from death, one of
Port Lincoln's galahs about to be clubbed to death.

The hapless galah about to meet its maker had previously been peppered with shot-gun pellets by willing gun-club volunteers, and this Port Lincoln Council's worker was merely delivering the *coup de gras.*

As local reporter Bronwyn Hurrell reported, galahs being shot and clubbed to death in the heart of Port Lincoln' because they are a nuisance.

Hundreds of the native parrots are being shot in trees and the survivors bashed to death when they fell to the ground'.

The local council had given open slather to gun club members and other registered gun owners to shoot the distinctive pink and grey parrots around sunset when they gathered in the trees. They were there because of the wheat harvesting season, when they gathered in their thousands to feed on spilled grain from huge grain trucks.

The Lincoln Council was also miffed that local Norfolk Island pines had also been stripped of foliage and residents had complained that as well as the ear-splitting squawking, the annual galah invasion also damaged their television aerials.

'But the safety of cull', reported Bronwyn Hurrell, 'has now been called into question after shotgun pellets rained onto the roof of a children's day-care centre during Tuesday night's shoot as children were being collected by relatives.

Kane Ferguson, 17, told *The Advocate* he had to shield his three-year-old brother from stray pellets.

Kane said he arrived at 6 pm to collect the little boy and heard a dozen shots and pellets hitting the roof of the Tiny Tafe preschool centre.

'The shooters were firing behind the railway station only 100 metres from the centre, as the last few children were being picked up. The shotgun pellets started hitting the bonnet of my car.

'So', Kane said, 'I had to shield my brother with my body when he got into the passenger side of the car.'

He later found his car's paintwork had been damaged by the pellets, and reported that to police.

But, incredibly, the town's notoriously gung-ho mayor, Peter Davis, defended the shoot and played down the risk to children.

'Life is a risk,' he said. 'Pellets raining down won't hurt you.'

'There is major damage being done by these birds. They are worth $2000 a pair on the open market, but the only thing you're allowed to do is shoot them – and whilst I'm here as mayor, shooting will continue.'

Police Sergeant Rene Steen confirmed the shooters did have permission to kill the galahs, and the incident at the preschool would be investigated.

Even the local RSPCA spokeswoman Mrs Sabine Kloss was less than hard-line on the galah slaughter, saying that her organisation's officers would 'look at photos from the shoot to decide whether to act', adding that while she thought culls should always be the last resort, she recognised 'they were sometimes necessary.'

GALAH'S OUT-FOXED.

What a difference a year makes!

On 18 January 1999, the *Adelaide Advertiser* revisited the Great Galah Shoot. However, the Port Lincoln Council was being coy about how the annual galah cull was being carried out following the controversy of the previous year. A local resident did say 'they were being trapped in the early morning and the late evening' when the native parrots settled to feed on parks and farmland. (How this was done, whether by a chlorine gas attack, shooting nets over the grazing birds and clubbing them out of the public gaze, or re-hiring the local gun clubs remained a secret.)

The local *Advocate* reporter, Hugh Morgan, wrote that at least the Kirton Port Lincoln Bowling Club had solved its problem in a cunning and unique way. For years the marauding galahs had flown to the club in the heart of the town and alighted to scratch and peck at the perfectly groomed grass of the bowling greens.

'That was until a bit of country logic came into play – and two stuffed foxes were put out to stand guard. The bowling club's assistant green's manager, Royce Kammermann, together with several members, thought up the fox guards.

'Now they fly over, take a look and see the foxes and keep going. We haven't had a problem with them since we've had these two on guard.'

Other devices had been tried, including plastic models of a hawk, but the galahs soon got used to them and still dug up the greens. Mr Kam-mermann pointed out that to stay ahead of the game, they did have to move the two stuffed foxes around the greens every couple of days.

The foxes have also been something of a tourist attraction, with visitors photographing them, apparently thinking they were real.

...

FAME IN A NAME

Few Australians get to have a verb created in their name, but the crusading left wing journalist, author and film maker, John Pilger received this unwelcome accolade from the British writer Auberon Waugh.

To Pilger:

'To pillage the truth, to treat a subject emotionally with generous disregard for inconvenient detail, to ham it up, always in the left-wing cause and always with great indignation. Wild accusations, conspiracy theories etc.

....

MUMBY THE WAITER

This intriguing snippet appeared in *The Sydney Morning Herald's* Column 8 in May 1999.

THEY were puzzled at the Dunbar House Restaurant, Watsons Bay, when they saw their ad in the *Australian Jewish News.* Who was "Mumby the waiter" and how could he help all those mums relax?

Relax with Mumby the waiter with a special Mother's Day Lunch

WHAT'S that? It should have read *Relax with Mum by the water...?* So what do they do with all the bookings asking for Mumby's relaxing service?

FRANK'S COCK...

And I am again indebted to *The Sydney Morning Herald* circa 1994 for this essential information. The story began with a warning...

This column's commitment to bringing you all the news that matters inevitably means that we occasionally run the risk of offending more delicate readers. Those who are easily upset should pass on to the next item immediately.

Well, news has arrived from the prestigious Toronto Film Festival of a triumph for Canadian film maker Mike Hoolboom, who will visit Australia next month for Melbourne's 'experimental' exposition of film, video and electronic media art.

The Toronto jury said: 'For its moving depiction of the universal human experiences of love and loss in the age of AIDS... the 1994 award was presented to Michael Hoolboom's film *Frank's Cock*.

The subtly titled film will be shown in Melbourne as part of a retrospective of Hoolboom's work, *The Agony Of Arousal*. No word from Frank yet on whether he was disappointed to learn Hoolboom's movie won in The Short Film category.

....

HOME GROWN IDIOTS

BROOKVALE IDIOT

Sydney's *North Shore Times* news crime column reported that a man walked into Brookvale McDonalds at 8:50 am, flashed a gun and demanded cash. The clerk turned him down because she said she couldn't open the cash register without a food order. When the man ordered a Big Mac, the clerk said they weren't available until 10.30 am as only the breakfast menu was on offer.

Frustrated, the man walked away.

ADELAIDE IDIOTS

Two men tried to pull the front off an ATM in Adelaide's Henley Street by running a chain from the machine to the bumper of their Toyota Landcruiser, but instead of pulling the front panel off the machine they pulled the bumper off their 4WD. Scared, and attracting attention from oncoming traffic, they left the scene and drove home, with the chain still attached to the machine, their bumper still attached to the chain, and with their vehicle's licence plate still attached to the bumper.

No, they did not use a stolen car.

WOLLONGONG IDIOT

A man walked into a 7-Eleven store, put a $20 bill on the counter and askedfor change. When the clerk opened the cash drawer, the man pulled a gun and asked for all the cash in the register, which the clerk promptly provided.The man took the cash from the clerk and fled, leaving the $20 bill on thecounter. The total amount of cash he got from the drawer?

Fifteen dollars.

ROOTY HILL IDIOT

Seems this guy wanted some beer pretty badly. He decided that he'd just throw a brick through a liquor store window, grab some booze and run. So he lifted the brick and heaved it over his head at the window with all his might.

The brick bounced back and hit the would-be thief on the head knocking him unconscious. Apparently, the liquor store window was made of Plexi-Glass. And the whole event was caught on videotape, which the store owner consequently sold for use on TV.

CAMPBELLTOWN IDIOT

As a female shopper exited the Campbelltown Kmart in Queen Street, a man grabbed her purse and ran. A shop assistant at Kmart called the police immediately and the woman was able to give them a detailed description of the snatcher. Within minutes, the police had apprehended him, trying to mingle in the shopping crowd on Queen Street. They put him in the car and drove back to the Kmart store. The thief was then taken out of the car and up to the Kmart front desk and told to stand there for a positive ID. To which he replied:

'Yes, Officer, that's her. That's the lady I stole the purse from.'

PORT MACQUARIE IDIOT

When a man attempted to siphon petrol from a motor home parked on a Port Macquarie street, he got much more than he bargained for. Police arrived at the scene to find an ill man curled up next to a motor home near spilled sewage. A police spokesman said that the man admitted to trying to steal petrol and plugged his hose into the motor home's sewage tank by mistake. He had tried to siphon the petrol by first sucking it up the hose.

The owner of the vehicle declined to press charges, saying that it was the best laugh he'd ever had.

....

THE TIME TRUE ART CAME TO BARMERA

The newspaper cutting is time worn, the date (alas) missing and the local paper unidentified. I expect the events described took place in the late 1970s or perhaps early 1980s. The report made me laugh out loud when I first read it. It still does.

Barmera is a small town in the Riverland region of South Australia, 220 kilometres north-east of Adelaide, and is primarily a farming town near the shores of Lake Bonney, a big natural freshwater lake discovered by the explorer Charles Bonney in in 1836.

A truck missed its cue at a theatre banquet in Barmera on Friday and brought down the house.

The 280 guests at the Bonney Theatre, out for an evening of wining and dining and musical style entertainment, sipped on their pre-dinner drinks unaware of the fate of the truck bringing the banquet.

Four hours later they were still sipping away – with disastrous consequences.

First of all, the truck bringing food had a series of flat tires. Then the trailer was damaged, spoiling the food.

Back in the Bonney Theatre the evening organised by the Apex Club went on regardless. A play, *A Bard's Banquet*, with players from the Arts Council of South Australia, was delayed to keep the acts in time with the scheduled banquet. But by 9 pm, with still no sign of the food, the curtain went up.

According to the arts Council touring manager, Mr J Maxwell, the famished but lubricated crowd was 'Rowdy, somewhat unruly and beyond caring for the finer points of theatre'.

An organiser mounted the centre stage to appeal for order, but was hit on the neck by a tomato. One of the audience quipped that the tomato should have been shared by the hungry audience.

Soup, hurriedly rustled up on the spot was served soon after but when empty, soup plates were hurled about the hall.

Mr Maxwell described the evening as 'a nightmare happening before my eyes'. He said climax came when his cast left the stage and reported seeing an over-amorous couple staging its own performance in the gallery overlooking the audience.

The second couple was later seen having intercourse between courses.

'It gave everyone something other than hunger to talk about,' Barmera resident and one of the guests Mrs C Rooney, said last night.

The caterer finally arrived at 11 pm. Some of the food was promptly eaten while the rest was disposed of as projectiles aimed at the actors on the stage.

The caterers did not charge. The guests had paid nine dollars. Drinks were extra. The St John Ambulance Brigade got about

$2000 from the epic fundraiser. 'I'm just grateful that my actors got through the night relatively unscathed,' Mr Maxwell said.

....

FROM FOOD TO FLATUS

I am indebted to Philip Clark's *Stay In Touch* column in *The Sydney Morning Herald* for this necessary and basic information.

A prominent Sydney specialist says that burps, farts and other manifestations of excessive wind are far more common that most people admit. Indeed, the average Australian probably farted about 15 times and produced about 700 millilitres of gas a day, according to the Chairman of the Gut Foundation, Professor Terry Bolan.

'I think many people have a problem – it is not necessarily abnormal, it's normal to have wind,' he told a Sydney luncheon, marking the release of a new anti-wind remedy, De-Gas,

Professor Bolin, the Associate Professor of Medicine at Sydney's Prince of Wales Hospital, said everything from fizzy drinks to anxiety and swallowing air while eating, drinking and talking could cause a buildup of wind in the stomach.

And a high-fibre diet and cruciferous vegetables, such as cabbage, cauliflower, broccoli and asparagus were notorious for producing gas. But the good news about intestinal gases was that 99 per cent had no smell, he said.

The bad news was that scientists were not yet clear about what made some gases offensive, so it was difficult to advise people what not to eat if they were to avoid offensive flatus.

The smell of coffee was derived from at least 100 compounds, and so it was 'simplistic to believe that faeces is any less complex than a coffee bean?' he said.

Professor Bolin went on to say that although wind and its associated problems of belching, bloating and farting troubled many Australians, they rarely caused serious problems. At worst they made people feel bloated and uncomfortable, and could result in 'social disadvantage'.

I am reminded of my late father's comment about the quality of home-brewed beer.

'Home-brewed beer is like farting – your own seems all right'!

....

And while we are on this explosive topic, it seems appropriate to end (as it were) with JC Abercrombie's verses on *The Silent Fart.*

> *Thou cowardly, furtive little sneak,*
> *Not a brave fart – more of a leak,*
> *Product of binges alcoholic,*
> *Rich rood or foul internal colic.*

> *O, slinking, timorous, bogus fart,*
> *Declare thyself for what thou art,*
> *Thou snivelling, deceptive cheat,*
> *That tiptoes out on stocking'd feet.*

For me, the rich stentorian bellow,
Like double bass, trombone or 'cello,
Result of pulses – bens or peas –
Bringer of intestinal ease.

Be resolute! In church – at table –
And fart as loud as you are able.
Divert your friends and make them merry
By trumpeting a loud 'Rasp-berry'.

Accept my counsel – and if you can –
With courage take – fart like a MAN!

....

THE GENTLE ART OF NOSE PICKING...

While on the topic of bodily orifices, a childhood friend, who later became a GP, sent me in 1989 a curious pamphlet titled NOSTRIL. Here is its rather singular masthead.

NOSTRIL

THE OFFICIAL ORGAN OF THE NATIONAL NOSTRIL NUDGERS ASSOCIATION OF AUSTRALIA

Published monthly   November 1989

A JOURNAL OF NEWS AND EVENTS FOR ALL LOVERS OF THE GENTLE ART OF NOSE PICKING

(SPECIAL SUMMER EDITION)

Here are two of its curiously nasal fixated articles.

AUSSIE NUDGER TAKES WORLD FREESTYLE MASTERS IN CLIFFHANGER IN UNITED STATES.

Veteran Tasmanian Noseworker Billy Pickers took on the best the world had to offer in Denver, Colorado last month in the World Masters Tournament and although unseeded quickly worked his way into the finals against Grand Master Plukstein of the USA. Before the largest crowd ever seen in the gigantic Nostratorium Pluckstein raced away to an early lead and at the end of the fifth chuka was in front with a handy 17 points. As they entered the first nostril of the sixth and final chuka it looked as though Billy would be returning to Australia with his hopes dashed. However Pickers in an amazing recovery double bogeyed the last extraction of the tenth nostril of the sixth chuka to bring him within striking distance. Plukstein was rattled and miscued the next extraction. Pickers replied with an effortless clean and jerk and the match was wide open. The game seesawed with an unprecedented 57 tie breakers with the crowd on their feet and hoarse. It then seemed almost an anticlimax when Pickers, with what seemed to be a consummate ease verging on the arrogant, slam dunked, to take the match.

Pickers finished the tournament with what all the experts would have thought to be an unattainable flick pick index of 3.5649. Well done Billy Pickers, Australia is proud of you.

DO CATS PICK THEIR NOSES?

In this regular feature from our veterinary correspondent we learn this month of some fascinating new research from Romania where scientists have been tudying the habits of domestic cats.

Because cats are amongst the most fastidious and clean of all animals one would not be altogether surprised to find that cats were concerned about nasal hygeine. However all attempts to observe this highly desirable trait in this species have proved to no avail. It seems that although cats are not exactly prudish in the performance of their bodily functions and grooming, the unexpected results of recent research in Romania have demonstrated that cats show an extraordinary degree of modesty when it comes to working the nostril. Studies on captive cats in total darkness, using infra red cameras show that the cat will only pick its nose under these conditions of absolute and complete darkness, and even then the cat will do it in a most furtive fashion as though at any minute it expects to be caught and be dealt some terrible punishment

Doing a little research on my own, I must bring to my nasal-enthusiast friend's attention to the following information from *The Australian*'s Melba column on 13 January 1998. Perhaps it might inspire another edition of *Nostril*.

Melba is pleased to be able to clear up a problem which has had world Jewry in a tizzy of late. It is OK to pick your nose on the Sabbath. And that's official. Apparently Israel's largest selling newspaper, *Yediot Ahronot*, mistakenly quoted leading ultra- orthodox Rabbi Ovadia Yosef saying it was forbidden to pick one's nose on the Sabbath because nose hairs might be pulled out, thus contravening a law against cutting hair on the holy day. However Yosef's aide, Amir Crispel, told reporters yesterday that the rabbi had actually ruled in favour.

I think we have almost certainly reached an excess of information on this topic.

....

AND FINALLY A WORD FROM AUSTRALIA'S NATIONAL CAPITAL

In February 2001 I was surprised to receive a letter from the National Capital Authority to mark the Centenary of Federation.

'In short, we are only approaching a very small number of Australians who have excelled in their particular field of endeavour to ask them to put in their own words what the National Capital, Canberra, means to them.

'Your response can be as short as you wish. You may wish to comment on the politics of Canberra, the unique layout of the city, the people or the weather.

'If possible could you write your response in your own hand on the page provided? We are considering a special publication for Centenary of Federation and these written responses would most certainly be included...'

Well, how could I refuse? I have never lived in Canberra, although I have visited it on professional and a personal level on many occasions. I invariably get lost, driving in the maze of circles created by the city's

American designer, Walter Burley Griffin. Even if I am familiar with where I am going, there is often a traffic diversion which spins me off into outer darkness. These were the days before satellite navigation. Now the unflappable, knowledgeable voice of Karen, my Apple Maps guide, would solve those problems. But not then.

I dutifully sent off my offering in my own execrable writing, but offer it here in print. I do not know whether I made it into the published book.

You can't go straight in Canberra
Thanks to Burley Griffin.
It's all circles, curves and roundabouts —
But the locals think it's Heaven.

The pollies can't keep straight as well,
But that's not Walter's fault.
Debate in the House is circular too.
And too often comes to nought.

9

FINAL ODDMENTS

THE BARD OF BALTI SPEAKETH

As democracy is perfected, the office of president represents, more and more closely, the inner soul of the people. On some great and glorious day the plain folks of the land will reach their heart's desire at last and the White House will be adorned by a downright moron.

(H L MENCKEN 1880-1956)

And as a gentle afterthought...

'Not all conservatives are uninformed, but most uninformed people are conservatives'. (J K GAILBRAITH)

....

FROM EVELYN WAUGH'S DIARIES...

Randolph Churchill went into hospital to have a lung removed. It was announced that the trouble was not 'malignant'. Seeing Ed Stanley in Whites [Club], on my way to Rome, I remarked that it was a typical triumph of modern medicine to find the only part of Randolph that was not malignant and remove it... (EVELYN WAUGH 1964)

....

A FEW THOUGHTS FROM VISIONARY AND COMEDIAN STEPHEN WRIGHT

When everything is coming your way, you're in the wrong lane. Hard work pays off in the future. Laziness pays off now.

Everyone has a photographic memory. Some just don't have film. For every action, there is an equal and opposite criticism.

The severity of the itch is proportional to the reach.

To steal ideas from one person is plagiarism – to steal from many is research.

A clear conscience is usually the sign of a bad memory.

If you must choose between two evils, pick the one you've never tried before.

If you think nobody cares about you, try missing a couple of payments.

Drugs may lead to nowhere, but at least it's the scenic route. 99 percent of lawyers give the rest a bad name.

42.7 percent of all statistics are made up on the spot.

....

ADOPTION – HOW OR WHEN TO BREAK THE NEWS...

In Australia, it has become almost impossible to adopt newly born children because of social changes that began with Gough Whitlam's Labor Government from 1972-75 which gave supporting benefits to single mothers.

That, coupled with the changes in public attitudes to the former 'disgrace' of a young woman becoming pregnant out of wedlock, meant that more choices were available to young single mothers.

What became Operation Babylift was put into effect by the United States Government in the closing months of the Vietnam War, from 4 April 1975. It was a mass evacuation of 10,300 infants and babies from South Vietnam, although the exact number of children has never been accurately assessed. The children were adopted by families in the United States and other countries including Australia, France, West Germany and Canada.

The first flight on 4 April was a disaster. It is not clear whether the lumbo jet was hit by North Vietnamese or Viet Cong rockets, but it crash-landed into a nearby rice paddy and burst into flames. Of the 300 people on board, the death toll included 78 children and 50 adults. Some 170 survived. Yet the airlifts continued for some weeks until military attacks on Saigon's Ton Son Nhut Airport made such flights impossible.

In Australia the influx of Vietnamese babies willingly adopted by child-less Australian couples signalled the virtual end of local adoptions – assisted by the changing social attitudes to single mothers already mentioned.

When my wife Ros and I adopted our two Australian-born sons in 1972 and 1975 we must have been one of the last families to do so locally. Overseas adoptions became the only practical alternative for Australian adopting parents. Official attitudes then were that the identities of the birth parents were to remain a secret and not allowed on the birth certificates. We decided that we would tell both our boys that they were adopted as soon as they could understand what that meant. Also, as they grew older and wanted to, we would help them try and find their birth mothers and fathers. Our elder boy, with Ros' help, did get his birth mother's name on his birth certificate, but decided to go no further. Our second son reacted with some alarm when finding his natural mother was mentioned, saying he was 'happy where I landed thanks'.

Not all adopted children knew of their adoption, sometimes with distressing psychological results when accidently discovered.

Because both Ros and I worked with ABC Radio's Social History Unit in Sydney, we were asked to take part in some documentary programs on adoption, and whether or when a child should be told of that fact. One of the researchers in our unit said that she had a nephew now in his early 20s who had been adopted and said she would ask him if he would agree to be interviewed about his attitudes to adoption. When she rang to ask him, there was a long pause, and he said, 'Well actually I would like to have more time to think about this because until you rang me, I didn't know I was adopted'! Oh dear.

Ros and I always believed that disclosure was the most honest approach, and that worked out well for us.

There are many stories now about adopted children who did make contact with their birth mothers and indeed fathers, with very happy results. Others were rejected, because the birth mother had entered into another relationship, had more children but had never told her partner about the baby she had relinquished for adoption. This remains a vexed area of course but to end on a lighter note, this question was dealt with by Tasmanian cartoonist Jon Kudelka with his customary wit and flair.

ALLEGED ACTUAL EXCERPTS FROM ROYAL NAVY AND MARINES OFFICER FITNESS REPORTS:

'His men would follow him anywhere, but only out of curiosity.'

'I would not breed from this officer.'

'He has carried out each and every one of his duties to his entire satisfaction.'

'He would be out of his depth in a car park puddle.'

'This medical officer has used my ship to carry his genitals from port to port, and my officers to carry him from bar to bar.'

'Since my last report he has reached rock bottom, and has started to dig.'

'She sets low personal standards and then consistently fails to achieve them.'

'He has the wisdom of youth, and the energy of old age.'

'Works well when under constant supervision and cornered like a rat in a trap.'

'This man is depriving a village somewhere of an idiot.'

....

ADVICE FROM A LAWYER FRIEND HOW TO HANDLE CROSS-EXAMINATION IN COURT

There are only three responses: 1 Not in my presence.

Not that I recall.

Can I have a glass of water?

....

'A CAMEL IS A HORSE DESIGNED BY A COMMITTEE'

Here are a few more:

'What is a committee? A group of the unwilling, picked from the unfit, to do the unnecessary.' (Richard Harkness, *The New York Times*, 1960.)

'A committee is a cul-de-sac down which ideas are lured before being quietly strangled.' (Anon.)

'A committee is a body that keeps minutes and wastes hours.' (Anon.)

....

'THE JOURNAL THE WORLD SWEARS BY'

So read the headline of Australian journalist David Dale's epistemological piece in *The Sydney Morning Herald* in 1986 in his regular column, *David Dales's America*. He and I are happy to run it again here.

Americans are so obsessed with politeness that it's hard to believe this country could sustain a regular magazine devoted entirely to insults. But *Maledicta – The Journal of Verbal Aggression* has been appearing now for 10 years and is the sole source of income for an editor and publisher, Dr Reinhold Aman.

Mind you, *Maledicta* comes out only once a year and has a mere 5000 subscribers, so we can hardly say the forces of 'Have a nice day' – have been vanquished. *Maledicta* does, however provide evidence that beneath the saccharine surface of American society there seethes a layer of fierce and creative malice.

Reinhold Anam says the ability to devise interesting insults is a sign of a mature community. He quotes Sigmund Freud: 'The first human who hurled curses instead of a weapon against his enemy was the founder of civilisation'. Aman sees his role in life as providing a scholarly chronicle of modern abuse.

Most Americans limit themselves to what Aman calls the dirty dozen insults, which are equally familiar to Australians and which show a preoccupation with sex or excretion. Catholic countries concentrate on blasphemy, he says, while Asian nations prefer ancestor abuse, and the Arab world has some nice twists on animals. 'May the fleas of 1000 camels invade your armpits'. The various sub-groups within the United States are doing their best to widen the vocabulary of vituperation.

For American blacks, the favourite epithet is an accusation of incest, which, in the usual pronunciation comes out sounding like 'mofo'.

Aman says it originated in Africa, and was brought to America by the slaves. There are variations on this theme, for example, 'mammy- jammer' and 'granny-jazzer', and in some combinations the term can indicate admiration rather than criticism, as in, 'he's one bad-ass mofo'.

Motherhood is a recurring theme in black abuse. You may hear black teenagers exchanging observations like, 'Your mother is like a birthday cake – everyone gets a piece', or 'Your mother is like a bowling ball – always getting laid in alleys'. But other members of the family are not immune. One of *Maledicta*'s contributors reported this line from a black schoolyard: 'Your brother is like a grocery store – he takes meat in the back'.

Californians have come up with some typically mellow maledictions, mostly synonyms for stupidity or drug-induced vagueness, as in 'air- head' or 'dipstick'.

People of Yiddish background have a style of insult that users the 'good news, bad news', formula: 'May you be famous – they should name a disease after you' or, 'May you receive three shiploads of gold – and they should be enough to cover your doctor's bills'.

There is also a Jewish tradition of using sarcastic questions to show comments judged to be inappropriate. Most often heard is, 'What am I, chopped liver'? But the range includes, 'Does a snake have knees? Does a chicken have lips? Does the Pope know Latin? Is the Pope Catholic? Is the hole close to a doughnut? Does a bear shit it in the woods? Is a pig's arse pork?'

Rural America offers a smorgasbord of scatology. 'He's so dumb he couldn't pour piss out of the boot with the directions printed on the heel: He can't tell owl's shit from putty without a map: Your breath's so foul it'd knock a buzzard off a manure wagon: He'd steal a rotten doughnut out of a bucket of snot: They are living so far out in the boondocks that you have to wipe the owl shit off the clock to see what time it is: He's got a smile that could sell used snuff.'

(Dale comments:' Don't these put Australian slang slingers to shame? Concoctions like, "as flash is a rat with a gold tooth", sound less impressive than we thought.')

Then there's the verbal aggression we develop in our professions. Well-informed contributors to *Maledicta* have catalogued kind terms doctors and nurses use when they think their patients can't hear or understand...

Albatross: a patient with multiple problems, unlikely to be cured (see Dump).

Banana: a jaundice patient.

Blimp: overweight patients.

Camel driver: a doctor of foreign origin, especially Middle East – also called flying carpet salesman.

Dump: patient nobody wants, who has been transferred to another hospital department.

FLK: a young patient with unusual appearance or behaviour – (stands for 'Funny Looking Kid').

Fruit ranch: Psychiatric unit – (also called 'International House of Pancakes').

Not even in the ballgame: senile or confused.

PPPPPT: A patient needing complex treatment (stands for 'Piss Poor Protoplasm Poorly Put Together').

SHPOS: a patient who gives trouble and his condition has worsened because of his failure to take care of himself (stands for 'Sub Human Piece of Shit').

Plumber: a urologist.

Soapbox derby syndrome: a rapidly progressing illness.

Three-toed sloth: a slow talking, slow acting patient, such as a degenerated alcoholic.

Aman calls *Maledicta*, 'The journal the world swears by'. He says its subscribers, from 28 countries, are mostly anthropologists, linguists and psychologists, with a with a smattering of doctors and journalists.

Aman's own specialities are linguistics and mediaeval literature, which he taught at the University of Wisconsin until 1974. At that stage he was told to seek employment elsewhere, because the university officials – 'those biodegradable nitwits in academia' as he calls them – regarded his research as undignified because i t had become focused on the offensive, the violent and scurrilous aspects of human languages over the past 5000 years.

So Aman continued his research privately and in 1977 issued the first edition of *Maledicta*, decorated with a hieroglyphic used on ancient Egyptian legal documents as a warning against breach of contract. It means, 'May you be fucked by a donkey'.

Publishing his journal and giving lectures around the world provided a meagre living and he wished there were more scholars like him. 'Every day around the world, tens of thousands of people are humiliated, demoted, fired, fined, jailed, injured, killed, or commit suicide because of insults, slurs, curses, threats, blasphemies, vulgarities and other offensive words', he says.

'Such events emphasise the importance of this type of language, and cry out for more research on verbal aggression and its effects.'

....

Australia may be lifting its game in the abuse stakes these days. I came across this little gem recently:

'May the hairs on your arse turn into fish-hooks, and rip the shit out of you.'

Which leads me to raise the tone of this debate and reflect on an era…

WHEN INSULTS HAD CLASS

(Some may already be known to the reader but not all I hope)

At a social gathering, Gladstone said to Disraeli: 'Sir, you will either die on the gallows or of the pox.' 'That depends, Sir,' said Disraeli, 'whether I embrace your policies or your mistress.'

'He had delusions of adequacy.' (Walter Kerr)

'He has all the virtues I dislike and none of the vices I admire.' (Winston Churchill)

'I have never killed a man, but I have read many obituaries with great pleasure.' (Clarence Darrow)

'He has never been known to use a word that might send a reader to the dictionary.' (William Faulkner – about Ernest Hemingway)

'Thank you for sending me a copy of your book; I'll waste no time reading it.' (Moses Hadas)

'I didn't attend the funeral, but I sent a nice letter saying I approved of it.' (Mark Twain)

'He has no enemies, but is intensely disliked by his friends.' (Oscar Wilde)

'I am enclosing two tickets to the first night of my new play. Bring a friend… if you have one.' (George Bernard Shaw to Winston Churchill), 'Cannot possibly attend first night, will attend second… if there is one.' (Winston Churchill, in response)

'I feel so miserable without you; it's almost like having you here.' (Stephen Bishop)

'He is a self-made man and worships his creator.' (John Bright)

'I've just learned about his illness… Let's hope it's nothing trivial.' (Irvin S Cobb)

'He is not only dull himself; he is the cause of dullness in others.' (Samuel Johnson)

'He is simply a shiver looking for a spine to run up.' (Paul Keating)

'In order to avoid being called a flirt, she always yielded easily.' (Charles, Count Talleyrand)

'Why do you sit there looking like an envelope without any address on it?' (Mark Twain)

'His mother should have thrown him away and kept the stork.' (Mae West)

'Some cause happiness wherever they go; others, whenever they go…' (Oscar Wilde)

'He uses statistics as a drunken man uses lamp-posts… for support rather than illumination.' (Andrew Lang)

'He has Van Gogh's ear for music.' (Billy Wilder)

'I've had a perfectly wonderful evening. But this wasn't it.' (Groucho Marx)

....

PROVERB FOR THE MILLENIUM

'The email of the species is more deadly than the male'. (Anon)

....

ODE TO AN ARTIFICIALLY INSEMINATED COW

This harks back to the last century when the artificial insemination of cattle was still something of a novelty. According to a veterinarian friend of my vintage, the following poem was authored by an unnamed West Australian Liberal politician travelling west-bound on the Indian Pacific Railway in the early 1980s.

(I should also explain that the indelicate and insensitive reference to the Australian Women's Land Army was also outdated, as the volunteer women who were recruited in 1942 to fill the labour gap when Japan entered World War II the previous year were long gone by the 1980s as they were disbanded on 31 December 1945!).

THE COW'S LAMENT

Though I've just given birth to a heifer,
And of milk and of pride I am full,
I am sad to relate That my lacteal state
Was not brought about by a bull.

I have never been naughty, I swear it,
In spite of the calf that I've borne.
Like Farmer Brown's tractor,
I'm Virgo Intactor
'Cause I've not had a bull by the horn.

How dreary the fields and the meadows,
he sheep yards are gloomy and grey,
As the one bit of fun
In the year's dreary run
Has by science been taken away.

I know that the farm is a business
In which we must all pull our weight.
But I'd pull and I'd pull For a strongly built bull,
For this phony arrangement I hate.

....

THE BRAVE FLASHER

This cartoon by JAK in the London Evening Standard made its way into my Oddments File while I was still working in London in the early 1960s.

THE UNHAPPY PLIGHT OF GUNTHER BURPUS

I hope this is true, but it was first published in Bremen, Germany, picked up by the Vancouver *Sun*, and reprinted in Britain's *Private Eye* last century, on the adventures of the remarkably named Gunther Burpus.

'In retrospect, I admit it was unwise to try to gain access to my house via the cat-flap', Gunther Burpus admitted to reporters in Bremen. 'I suppose that is the reason they are called cat-flaps, rather than human-flaps is because they are too small for people, and perhaps I should have realised that.

Burpus, a 41-year-old gardener from Bremen was relating how he had become trapped in his own front door for two days, after losing his house keys. 'I got my head and shoulders through the flap, but became trapped fast around the waist. At first it all seemed rather amusing, I sang songs and told myself jokes. But then I wanted to go to the lavatory. I began shouting for help, but my head was in my hallway so my screams were muffled.

'After a few hours a group of students approached me but, instead of helping, they removed my trousers and underpants, painted my buttocks bright blue, and stuck a daffodil between my cheeks. Then they placed a sign next to me which said, *Germany resurgent, an essay in street art – please give generously*' and left me there.

'People were passing by and, when I asked for help, they just said, "very good, very clever!" and threw coins into my trousers. No one tried to free me. In fact, I only got free after two days because a dog started licking my private parts and an old woman complained to the police. They came and cut me out, but arrested me as soon as I was freed.

'Luckily they've now dropped the charges, and I collected over DM3000 in my underpants, so the time wasn't completely wasted'.

....

STIFF PUNISHMENT
Source: Roger Woddis

In Johannesburg a white policeman who exposed himself to three black women was killed when he tripped over his trousers and fell in front of a train.

In heaven now, a man of worth Is
playing on his harp,
And how he came to leave this earth Is
worthy of Tom Sharpe.

He was so keen on sharing love, He
was prepared to show.
In homage to his God above,
The naked man below.

He tripped and stumbled to his doom.
The train it failed to stop: Alas!
When base desires consume
A fine, upstanding cop.

No stranger he to civil strife,
Nor acts considered rash.
But thus exposed, his blameless life
Was over in a flash.

He was a man who stood apart,
And lonely on his beat:
There were dark longings in his heart,
And trousers round his feet.

....

THE NAUGHTY TURTLE

This story appeared in the English language *Jakarta Post* in 1966.

The Naughty Turtle

BANDUNG Nov.18 (Antara News Agency)

A turtle was put to death here for having attacked a man's genitals. The incident happened when En (27) was having a move in the Tjilapundung River with his body partly immersed in the water.

People saw En suddenly grimace with pain by the turtle's bite. En asked the people who came to his rescue not to kill animal immediately because he wanted to revenge himself first.

But his rescuers, upon seeing blood dripping from En's wound, were terrified. They caught the turtle and killed the naughty animal. Then they took En to the nearest clinic.

The scene of the happening was behind the office building of the state electricity company PLN and in broad daylight.

En is now fully recovered from his injury after having undergone a light surgery. On 16 November last he celebrated his marriage.

A great relief to all concerned I would have thought.

....

A TRIUMPH OF BRITISH DIPLOMACY

I would like to end this eclectic collection amassed over a long life with a personal favourite. It has been around the traps a bit, and I have seen it published elsewhere. It does have the virtue of being authenticated by impeccable sources.

The following note was written during the World War II by the British Ambassador to Moscow, Sir Archibald Clerk Kerr, to Lord Pembroke of the Foreign Office. It was released under the Freedom of Information Act on 25 February 2000:

My dear Reggie,

In these dark days man tends to look for little shafts of light that spill from Heaven. My days are probably darker than yours, and I need, my God I do, all the light I can get. But I am a decent fellow, and I do not want to be mean and selfish about what little brightness is shed upon me from time to time. So I propose to share with you a tiny flash that has illuminated my sombre life and tell you that God has given me a new Turkish colleague whose card tells me that he is called Mustapha Kunt.

We all feel like that, Reggie, now and then, especially when Spring is upon us, but few of us would care to put it on our cards. It takes a Turk to do that.

Sir Archibald Clerk Kerr,

H.M. Ambassador

And that, it seems is that.

Tim Bowden

H.M. EMBASSY
MOSCOW

Lord Pembroke
The Foreign Office
LONDON

6th April 1943

My Dear Reggie,

In these dark days man tends to look for little shafts of light that spill from Heaven. My days are probably darker than yours, and I need, my God I do, all the light I can get. But I am a decent fellow, and I do not want to be mean and selfish about what little brightness is shed upon me from time to time. So I propose to share with you a tiny flash that has illuminated my sombre life and tell you that God has given me a new Turkish colleague whose card tells me that he is called Mustapha Kunt.

We all feel like that, Reggie, now and then, especially when spring is upon us, but few of us would care to put it on our cards. It takes a Turk to do that.

Sir Archibald Clark Kerr,
H.M. Ambassador.